Post Modernist Delegation to English Language Teaching

The Quixotic Deluge

Post Modernist Delegation to English Language Teaching

The Quixotic Deluge

Nandini Sahu

AUTHORSPRESS

Worldwide Circulation through Authorspress Global Network
First Published 2005
by Authorspress

E-35/103, Jawahar Park
Laxmi Nagar, Delhi-110 092

e-mail: authorspress@yahoo.com

Typeset in NewCenturySchlbk by Chitra Computers

Post Modernist Delegation to English Language Teaching: The Quixotic Deluge
ISBN 81-7273-287-2

Printed in India at Tarun Offset, Delhi.

Preface

"Writing about writing?" My friend asked me quizzically when I started working on this book. "Well, sort of," I confessed, "or at least about writing perfectly. Speaking flawlessly, with good accent, reading voraciously, and about presenting yourself amiably." This slightly periphrastic exchange prompted me for the publication of this book, *Post Modernist Delegation to English Language Teaching: The Quixotic Deluge* based on a collection of articles presented in a National Level Workshop on 'Importance of Language Studies in technical Education' that I conducted in IACR Engineering College in Rayagada, Orissa, on 26-27 February 2005. This book pulls together a number of my ruminations about the pleasures and perils of the written and the spoken word, and about the ultra-modern techniques of English language teaching. It is a book that would appeal only the elite mass who themselves are devoted to writing, research and the travelogues in reading.

Over the years I have written a number of articles and reflections on various subjects and most of them happen to be on literature having deserved a wider and enduring readership. In this book I feel I am devoting more on collecting from life as much as from the written text, having a quixotic quest with which I conducted the workshop. Most of the essays are rather less anecdotal, rueful pieces musing on language as a vehicle of thought, and on expression of the 'self' through language as well as body language as the quintessential need of one and all.

On the day of the workshop, while entering the conference hall for the inaugural session, I was mildly surprised by the cynicism of somebody's question who asked me if it wasn't all a waste of time to conduct a linguistic workshop in a technical institute. "What does a conference like this actually achieve?" he wanted to know. This was remarkably a utilitarian approach to the occasion, and I suppose I could have responded by pointing out to the many parallel seminars being run by government and private organisations to attract investments, or the sessions on disaster management that had been added in the wake of tsunami, or that English is an international language, and it is a must for us to learn to go global. But I preferred to make a larger point: that the real value of a conference lies in the conferring. Language determines a person's education. The proper use of language at a proper place is a sign of a person's level of learning. Trained to be an expert in our branch studies but failing to communicate properly, a person cannot think of the cooperation of others and self-development which is highly essential for success.

Engineering graduates require an ever-increasing range of skills to maintain relevance with the global environment of the new millennium. Communication skills are a vital component of this, recognised by academia and industry alike. English language skills are also important given its widespread status across the globe as a lingua franca. Indeed, multilingual skills are considered a salient element in the make-up of the new global engineer. English for specific purposes focuses the learner's attention on the particular terminology, and communication skills are required in the international professional field. The idea of the workshop was to create an awareness among the faculty and students to the fact as to how communicative skills, interpersonal skills, language studies form an integral part of teaching, research and development in technical as well as general studies and re-discover the newer methods of teaching language and literature through the effective use of a Language Laboratory by making experimentations on pronunciation practice, phonetics and linguistics. Also how a Communication Laboratory is most required for grooming the students in interpersonal skills, communicative skills, personality development, interview preparations and technical presentations. This purpose can be solved by using technically proficient software like Language Modification tools, Language Correction tools, Phonetic Recognition tools, etc.

The Global Citizen

Globalisation directly influences the industry's needs; a global citizen must be able to easily cross national and cultural boundaries. This in turn directly affects education, so a common code for communication is required. Those education institutions, which meet the language requirements for the new global citizen, will be ready to face the new millennium. Engineers can relate the same theories of mathematics, of mechanics and technology, but the modern engineer must also be able to communicate effectively in a shared tongue. English has become the ascendant language internationally, being the most widespread. This will influence the language of communication between professionals internationally. In this age of globalisation, the number of international projects is increasing, and cross-cultural communication and collaboration is on the rise. English is cited as the major language of international business, diplomacy, and science and the professions. It is through this method that English appears to be spreading the most, compared to past centuries that were dominated by immigration and settlement, such as Canada, the USA and Australia. English is the prime means for communication, and can often serve as the global language between two people from two different cultures, wherein English is not the native tongue.

Communicative Skills

Communication is a range of purposeful behaviour, which is used with intent within the structure of social exchanges, to transmit information, observations, or internal states, or to bring about changes in the immediate environment. Verbal as well as non-verbal behaviours are included, as long as some intent, evidenced by anticipation of outcome can be inferred. While communicating with someone, we can use the following units to weigh and consider:

1. Identify the speaker(s), eg., TV presenters, interviewers, interviewees, etc.
2. Aim of communication, e.g., explaining, reminding, asking, protesting, informing, recounting, etc
3. What is the speaker's verbal manner? e.g., angry, patient, insistent, confrontational, etc.
4. Describe speaker's physical manner, facial expressions, gestures, body language, etc.
5. Who is the communication aimed at ? (specific individuals/categories of people)
6. What is the speaker's relationship to the person/people identified?

PRESENTING A TECHNICAL PAPER

Technical presentations are a must for the engineers throughout their career and also during interviews. A presentation consists of two parts: the things you tell your audience and the things you show them. Generally, you will tell your audience your findings and why they are important, and show them photographs, charts, and diagrams to reinforce what you are telling them.

PRONUNCIATION

Of late, Indian writing in English has become a genre of international interests. Indians have learnt the colonial language perfectly since the days of Tagore, Dutt Family Album, maturing with Nissim Ezekiel, Jayanta Mahapatra, A.K. Ramanujam, R.Parthasarathy, G. Sarat Chandra, Anita Desai, Kamala Das and modern poets/ writers like Niranjan Mohanty, Bibhu Padhy, Vikram Seth, Salman Rushdie, Manju Kapur, Arundhati Roy, Manoj Das and many more.

But, do Indians emulate the British tongue and stylistics along with the language? About Indian English, poet Nissim Ezekiel writes in the poem, 'A Very Indian Poem in Indian English':

> I am standing for peace and non-violence
> Why world is fighting fighting
> Why all people of world
> Are not following Mahatma Gandhi
> I am simply not understanding.
> Ancient India wisdom is 100 per cent correct
> I should say even 200 per cent correct.
> But modern generation is neglecting
> Too much going for fashion and foreign thing.

Here the post satirises on the natives who tend to destroy the beauty of the language. This suggests that we must learn the proper use and pronunciation of any language when we opt the spoken form of it as the medium of instruction, English in our case, the most widely acclaimed world language. In the Communicative English classes, we emphasize on Linguistics, Phonetics and Intonation, use software like the Oxford Talking Dictionary and the Random House Talking Dictionary, Vocabulary Wizard, Talk It. When the students go for presentations, prior to that we have voice recording sessions, testing of pronunciation through Talk It, presentation sessions in mirror fitted cabins, so that the students achieve perfection.

Interview Tips

A recent report from Melbourne, Australia, stated that employers now seek graduates with skills beyond the standard paper degree; this includes an excellent level of skills in:

— Communication

— Decision making

— Teamwork

— Awareness of the social implications of their discipline's developments.

— Management skills.

— Understanding of other points of view and other cultures.

— Confidence and competence to work in international environments.

Other areas identified in the report included competencies in business acumen, marketing and public relations. Having the most knowledge was not as important as getting the work done in the most effective manner. Employers gave considerable value on graduates acquiring a diverse set of skills in differing work environments. Thus, keeping in view the global requirements, in the curriculum of English, we include interview tips sessions, mock interviews, through which the pupils get an idea about the interviews they would face after they graduate. The mock interviews include the following:

	Marks	*15*	*10*	*05*	*Percentage*
1.	Educational Qualifications	Good	Average	Inadequate	
2.	Professional Competency	Good	Average	Deficient	
3.	Communicative Skills	Excellent	Good	Bad	
4.	Body Language	Good	Acceptable	Bad	
5.	Aptitude	Excellent	Mediocre	Bad	
6.	Self-Confidence	Vibrant	Manageable	Inferior	
7.	Presentation Skills	Optimum	Good	Average	
8.	Eye Contact	Positive	Manageable	Negative	
9.	Pronunciation/ Accent	Excellent	Manageable	Bad	
10.	Written				

(Contd...)

(Contd...)

	Communication	Proficient	Medium	Bad
11.	Basic Leadership Quality	Team-Builder	Team-Manager	Follower
12.	Sociability / Adaptability	Good	Average	Bad
13.	General Awareness	Uptodate	Medium	Bad
14.	Personality	Magnetic	Influencing	Weak
15.	Interpersonal Skills	Good	Mediocre	Bad

I want to make a general distinction between writing a language and writing in a language, speaking a language and speaking in a language. There is a sense in which the latter distinction is a particularisation of the former. Thus, in order to learn the latter, one has to make conscious efforts to learn the language specifically, because, the Oriental tongue is not acquainted with English, as with the mother tongue. For this reason English may not be learnt as a theoretic language like earlier times, a language laboratory must be supplemented to teaching English—be it Communicative English, Linguistics or Literature.

Language and communication skills are recognised as important elements in the education of the modern generation, including English for specific purposes. Yet, there seems to be limited implementation of English courses globally, despite its current lingua franca status. Those institutions that have already implemented multilingual and communication elements will be at the forefront of providing the demands of industry and society.

The incorporation of several components of the fundamentals of emotional intelligence in education will facilitate advanced communication skills. However, given the traditionalist nature of many engineering curricula, this may take some time before change is evidenced. The incorporation of language and communication improvement courses is an important element of continuous learning, and will ultimately contribute to the process of lifelong learning.

This should in turn facilitate advancements in engineering and, indeed, engineering education through streamlining fundamental communication skills. This, specifically, was the theme of the workshop, which was elaborated by me as the Organising Secretury as well as the Keynote Speaker, Prof. M.L.Das.

I thank all the contributors for their luminous studies and keen interest on the subject. The motive that worked behind the workshop was to give a fresh look into the corpus of ELT, especially after the post-modern times during which period it has no doubt won milestones of sporadic victory, but has often failed in terms of an original voice due to lack of a clear-cut objective to fall back upon. The English teachers before the last two decades had a different agenda on their hands, and their literary efforts gave a motive and urgency to their handling of the language and literature classes. Slowly in our times a distant Indian ethos emerged calling for a radical identity and a well defined focus which have so far eluded the modern English teachers. In the meanwhile, English as a language of communication has acquired a distinct status on its own right, not as a medium transplanted from outside as an adopted language, but as a spontaneous growth within a socio-cultural matrix, where we may truly belong and seek to fulfil ourselves, by modes of expression and manners of speech. Self-expression is the basic motive and within that limit one may seek to ply one's trade which is to understand and communicate within a congenial psychological climate. And the aim is to interpret the condition of man above the barriers of speech and hindrance of geographical boundaries, to project a brighter image of the speaker among the chosen couriers of the globe.

As I have discussed earlier, all the articles in the book deal with the art of perfect speaking, presenting, perceiving and writing. I am thankful to the contributors for their keen interest on the subject.

Nandini Sahu

Acknowledgements

This textbook builds on the work of many teachers and researchers. Its most immediate and obvious debts are due to all the authors, Prof. M.L.Das, Dr. C.D.Panda, Dr. K.B.Patel, Mr. G.C.Patro, Prof. Bharambar Badhai, Dr. C.K.Sadangi, Mrs. Sanchita Choudhury, Mr.Sanjeev Pattnaik, Mr. Atish Sarkar, Dr. Smita Sinha, Mr.S.K.Mishra, Ms. Tripti Mund, Mrs. Jayshree Nanda, Dr. Gobardhan Sahu, Mr. Manas Ranjan Mishra, Prof. Padmini Sahu, Ms. Deepanjali Mishra, Mrs. Susama Panda, Prof.P.N. Singh, Prof. P.K.Subudhi, Mr. P.C.Mishra, Mr. R.C.Thakur, Mr. Gouri Shankar Patnaik and Ms. Shalini.

On this occasion, I seize upon the rare privilege of thanking Mr. M.K.Palo, the Secretary of IACR, who is the only strong force behind my success in the workshop, who is my friend, philosopher and guide over here, who hardly ever gives me an opportunity to express my gratefulness, and who prefers to be the oxygen in the life-giving water.

I would like to express my eternal gratitude to Dr. C.D.Panda, Chairman, IACR, Mr. S.C.Panda, Director (Admn.), IACR, Prof. B.N.Panda, Principal, IACR, Mr. B.Ramprasad, Director (Finance) and Mr. R.P.Mohapatra, Director, IACR, Dr. I.D.N. Prasad, Dean of Students' Affairs, IACR, who have guided and helped me at every step during the conduct of the workshop and later on encouraged me to publish the papers in a book form.

I also take the privilege of giving my special thanks to Prof. R.K. Mishra, Vice Chancellor, BPVT, who had inspired me to conduct the workshop and guided me at every step.

In course of my research on the topic, I had the benefit of inspiration from Prof. Niranjan Mohanty, Prof. P.C.Kar, Prof. Kalidas Mishra, Prof. Pashupati Jha, Prof. E.Raja Rao, Prof. Dilip Das, Prof. Soubhagya K. Mishra, Prof. D.D.Sahu, Prof. Anasuya Das, Prof. R.N.Panda, and all my teachers. I wish to thank them all.

I express my heartfelt gratitude to my parents, in-laws, sisters, brothers-in-law, and my fond husband, who have been highly ambitious about my academic career. I thank my son Partho whose possession makes me complete.

I would love to give my special thanks to Dr. Kcherry Sudarshan, Managing Director, Authorspress, whose relationship with me is beyond that of just an author and a publisher, who has been a very good friend since the beginning.

I would also thank the teaching and non-teaching staff members and students of IACR for their active help, support and inspiration.

Last but not least, I feel elevated to thank Him on Whose Benign Hands I dedicate this book.

Nandini Sahu

List of Contributors

1. Prof. M.L.Das
University Professor of English (Retired)
Former Vice-Chancellor,
Vinoba Bhave University,
Hazaribag
Jharkhand State.

2. Bhramarbar Badhai
(Lecturer-in-Humanities)
Utkalmani Gopabandhu
Institute of Engineering,
Rourkela, Orissa

3. Dr. Gobardhan Sahu
Department of English
D.A.V. College,
Titilagarh – 767033

4. Dr. Chhayakanta Sarangi
Department of English
D.A.V.College, Titilagarh
Dist-Bolangir (Orissa)

5. Dr. C.D.Panda
Department of Economics,
Gunupur College
Rayagada, Orissa

6. Prof. Padmini Sahu
   Dept. of English
   Aska Department College
   Aska, Orissa

7. G.C. Patro, Dy. Dir.
   DTE&T Orissa,
   Cuttack & Chairman,
   ISTE Orissa Section

8. Prof. P.K.Subudhi
   Asst. Professor & Head
   Department of ECE & EEE
   IACR, Rayagada

9. Prof. P.C.Mishra
   Asst. Professor
   Department of CSE, IT& MCA
   IACR, Rayagada, Orissa

10. Prof. P.N.Singh
    HOD (CSE/IT/MCA)
    IACR, Rayagada, Orissa

11. Mr. Manas Ranjan Mishra
    Department of English
    Gopalpur College
    Ganjam, Orissa

12. Dr.Nandini Sahu
    Prof. Of English
    IACR, Rayagada,
    Orissa

13. Mr. S.K.Mishra
    B.Sc. (Ag.), M.A. (Eng.)
    Asst. Agriculture Officer,
    Rayagada.

14. Ms. Sanchita Choudhury
Lecturer in English
Padmanava College of Engineering
Rourkela, Orissa

15. Atish Chandra Sarkar (B.E., MBA)
Rourkela

16. Dr. Jayashree Nanda
Lecturer in Education
Kunja Bihari College,
Barang, Khurda,

17. Dr. Kunjaban Patel
Reader in English
S.D. Women's College
Rajgangpur-770017
Orissa.

18. Ms. Tripti Mund
Lecturer in English
National Institute of Science and Technology
Berhampur, Orissa

19. Mrs. Susama Panda
C/o. Mr. S.C.Panda
Director (Admn.), IACR
Rayagada

20. Ms. Deepanjali Mishra
Lecturer in English
Gandhi Institute for Technical Advancement
Bhubaneswar,
Orissa

21. Dr. Smita Sinha
Faculty Member, Department of Linguistics
Berhampur University,
Berhampur, Orissa.

22. Prof. Subash Chandra Pati
Department of English
B.R.M. College, Bhuban
Dhenkal-17, Orissa

23. Mr. Gouri Shankar Patnaik
B.Tech (Information Technology)

24. Mr. R.C.Thakur
Department of English
IACR, Rayagada, Orissa

25. Ms. Shalini
B.Tech (Second Semester)
IACR, Rayagada, Orissa

26. Mr. Sanjeev Kumar Pattnaik
Disha Learning Services
Rourkela, Orissa

Contents

Introduction

Twenty-five essays that constitute this volume explore various aspects of English language teaching, functional and communicative approaches to syllabus design and material production, different kinds of English and their different uses in language and literature classes, on personality development, inter-personal skills, linguistics, phonetics and the application of linguistic theories to the study of literature.

In his highly perceptive essay, M.L. Das shows as to how language has been an ever-growing ever-changing phenomenon, changing under the impact of social and technological changes, and the users of language have always been adapting to the effective, optimum use of language, be it with the help of language laboratories or learning in the classrooms or trying it in different kinds of media. The twenty-first century man, riding the crest of great technological and scientific advancements, has started experiencing formidable changes in the means and modes of communication. This phenomena has been variously described as microelectronic or the communication or information revolution. Its impact on the society has been regarded as analogous to the impact the railways had on the mid-nineteenth century. As a matter of fact, all technological changes affect the style and shape of life in societies. These also influence the courses of communication which ultimately stamp their effects on language and literature.

Dr. K.B. Patel calls attention to how the Second Language Teaching (SLT) in the last few years has already undergone several revolutions. We, the English teachers in India, do not seem to be aware of such revolutionary changes, what to speak of applying those new ideas in the Second Language Classroom (SLCs), we continue to teach in a social vacuum. Hence, even after several years of serious and sincere teaching, the Second Language Learners (SLLs) fail to communicate in real-life discourse situations. The result is either break of communication or miscommunication, which, instead of solving problems, often create new ones at the social and cultural levels. In a multilingual country like India, English is the lingua franca through which future citizens, who are being groomed in the Second Language Classrooms, are going to discuss and sort out the problems of the society. The teachers of English must not, therefore, forget the vital role they are going to play in helping learners master the English language.

Smita Sinha states that effective communicative skills are the essential attributes of an impressive personality. Most of the existing language teaching methodologies emphasise only on the correct formation of grammatical sentences and interpretation of texts. They focus on developing the listening skill, speaking skills, reading skills and writing skills only. Very little attention has been given to the communicative skills as a tool for personality development and interpersonal skills. Communication does not mean only to speak and write. It has broad connotation. It means to articulate properly and to create an impact on the hearer.

In her sharp and insightful critical survey, Nandini Sahu attempts to make a research on the newer methods of teaching. The classroom is a microcosm of the world, dealing with every subject like literature, science, technology, biographies, natural history, Buddhist self-help books, the *Bible*, spiritual texts, mathematics, philosophy, travel literature, manuals of household, computing, geography, physiognomy, music. But teachers should be formal, objective in their approach to each subject, professionalism upholding the importance of the job over personal concerns. In spite of whatever feelings the teachers might be experiencing or distractions they might be facing those should always take a backseat to performance and the task at hand. On the whole, teaching provides us with a depth of tragic understanding of life.

Mr. G.C. Patro rediscovers the concept of living with intelligence. Life is intelligent undoubtedly. Taking the examples from the living world, everything is blessed with intelligence. The awareness of intelligence may not be with the lower lives as in human beings. The unawareness of intelligence or the awareness of unintelligence is visible in man, may it be man, animal or plants. Probably nobody has ever heard addressing a plant as idiot; or ever seen a cat, dog, or so behaving idiotically excepting human beings.

Tripti Mund brings out the salient features of intercultural differences. In today's scenario one of the roots of success is to be sensitive to the intercultural differences. We belong to several cultures. In the micro perspective each individual has his own cultural identity which is communicated through the coordination of his body language and his manner of speaking. An individual identity always has the reflection of his own culture in the city or country to which he belongs. Culture as a whole is the shared system of symbols, beliefs, attitudes, values, expectations, and norms for behaviour.

Sanjeev Pattnaik throws light on how personality development and interpersonal skills play a very vital role in each and every aspect of our life, whether it is personal or professional. Or in other words, it is a prerequisite for success. And for this success communicative skill plays an important role. Effective communication is a short-cut to distinction. This communication gives us an edge over others. It is this communication which makes people successful and brings them to the limelight. We talk of any group of people or from any profession it is mainly the communication which has given them the distinct edge, whether it a successful businessman, or a politician or the babas or any other person.

G.Sahu holds the theory that experimental phonology represents an attempt to draw together at least three research styles: experimental phonetics, experimental psychology and phonological theory. This move is not always free of the implication that phonology is speculative and that evidence obtained experimentally is superior to any other kind of evidence.

Manas Ranjan Mishra sums up very briefly but succinctly that the pattern of English teaching and learning in India since a long period of time has been traditional in nature. The purposes of teaching English in the past aimed to get the students acquainted with the texts which have something to convey. But in the present set-up where without English we feel helpless, one needs to acquire it with little effort. These professionals encouraged new phenomena towards study of language, which gained immense importance with the growth of the IT sector. The term 'Communicative English' has taken hold because of the revolution in the IT sector.

C.K. Sarangi in his socio-linguistic study shows that language is a form of human social behaviour. Therefore, it is natural that there should be varieties of languages. Communities split up into groups and each group displays differences of behaviour. Language reflects these differences. The primary function of language is to convey ideas from one person to another, but these ideas may be information, command or request.

B.B. Badhai makes a detailed comparative study of communicative method of teaching. He proposes a graded pattern of imparting academics so as to make it learner-friendly. Language being the extant and common medium, communicative method of teaching aims at simplifying things at the linguistic level so as to make things coherent. Further, cogency of thought and expression is achieved through various interactive methods of putting the content in order to acquaint the learner with the basics.

In another insightful paper, Dr.C.D. Panda shows how language use in multilingual and multicultural India is naturally diverse. Although each state in India is carved out based on the dominant language of the region, any school or work environment is also multilingual and multicultural. In such a complex environment, language of knowledge and the culture language may come into conflict with each other and hinder inter-community and intra-community communication.

Susama Panda rightly chips in that technical field and language both are intricately intertwined and bring forth the latent personality in ourselves. The prerequisites of presentation of our national talents and technical skills are well communication skills and proper interaction. Presentation of national skills at an international conference demands the foundation to be very strong in English.

Subash Pati thinks that the process of teaching English in India poses a major problem—whether to teach it as a language or a literature. Unless a student has a special interest he seems to be reluctant to read English as a literature. Majorities of students prefer to read it as a language and an effective means of self-expression. A teacher cannot ignore this aspect while teaching English. Quite naturally, we come to the conclusion that we should have to devise effective ways of teaching English, which will increase the language proficiency of students both in writing and in speaking.

Padmini Sahu considers that, like human beings, language may also be considered a living organism, which is subjected to both decay and development. Total vocabulary of an individual is not constant at any age and time in his life-span. It is constantly subjected to change. The new experiences may bring subtle changes in the individual's vocabulary by adding some items to his vocabulary. The words that are in his total vocabulary may get deleted because of lack of opportunities for him to use those items, or because of the circumstances, which demand and maintain the use of such items, do not exist anymore, or some of the words of the total stock may acquire new meanings.

S.K.Mishra holds linguistics as the science and art of language. The great edifice structure that the language is, it cannot be as it is without the art and architecture it has at present; and the architecture is nothing but the linguistics that has about such an architectural work high and grand-like language. To put it differently, the speaker's knowledge of the structure of a language is his linguistic competence, and the way in which he uses it is his linguistic performance. Whereas competence is a set of principles, which a speaker masters, performance is what a speaker does.

Deepanjali Mishra shares her classroom experience as to how Hinglish is a form of English that echoes a more polite and formal age. The previous longing to acquire a British or American accent has disappeared along with the sneers once prompted due to mispronunciation. Now, whenever an Indian word or an idiosyncrasy is being discussed the standard reaction is to laugh and say, "We are like that only."

P.N. Singh opines that English is an increasingly important global language of communication.. Countries that wish to compete in the global economy have a keen awareness of the need for competent English speakers in business, politics and education. Therefore, there is a steady demand for English language in engineering colleges also. It should be for the first two semesters in the course as a foreign language or second language. Students can be encouraged by expressing them need of the language and arranging extempore, debates, group discussions, personality development classes and writing fictions in English to get more command over the language.

Jayshree Nanda draws the importance of English language for the personality development of technical students. Language is not a natural phenomenon; it is a creation of man's social needs. Hence human beings depend on language, as they depend on air, water, and the earth around it for their own existence. Language is an extremely complex and highly versatile code that is used to communicate our thoughts, desires and experiences to other persons. Language and human culture are intimately related, and the one is indispensable to the other. When man's attention is turning increasingly towards analysing his culture, it is natural that he should attempt to examine in detail the means of communication, which is essential to his society.

P.K. Subudhi and Prof. P.C.Mishra hold the view that recent years have shown an explosion of interest in using computers for English language teaching and learning. A decade ago, the use of computers in the English language classroom was of concern only to a small number of specialists. However, with the availability of multimedia computing and the internet, the role of computers in English language instruction to Low English Proficient (LEP) students has now become an important issue for large numbers of English language teachers throughout the world.

Sanchita Choudhury opines that personality grooming is a basic and essential need of the hour. This is meant for one and all. Just like our daily course of staple food alone is not sufficient to give us the necessary nutrition to sustain and we need to take vitamins as supplements, similarly to cope with today's competitive world and be successful, traditional courses of education need to be supplemented with special training on personality development. In order to sustain and succeed in this competitive world, the naive form of personality must be groomed well so as to make it fit for certain specific environment and purpose. In fact, personality is not merely a reflection of the outer self.

Atish Sarkar focuses on the influence of situational factors on communication in the practical life of engineers. An engineer is required to perform as a leader. So in this process of transformation, a technocrat is required to work with people, understand and develop interpersonal skills, build relationship and network with people in various hierarchical positions, social stature and intellectual levels. Engineers also need to command and motivate a team of people having diverse background and qualifications.

Needless to say here that whatever be one's technical skills, without a command on communication and human skills, success is likely to remain an unachieved dream in life.

Gouri Shankar Patnaik highlights the relevance of English as a passage to global citizenship. English has come to represent modernisation and development, and, as a link language, it has acquired international roles over the years. Some other reasons for the dominance of English around the world are its propensity for acquiring new identities, its power of assimilation, its manifestation in a range of sects, and its provision of a flexible medium for literary and other types of creativity across languages and cultures.

Shalini holds that a technocrat has the accurate medium of communication as English. An organisation is a place where people are working at different levels. They all have there own opinions and approaches. All the different people must be joining hands together for a common profit. In today's world of technical advancement a lot of importance is given to effective communcation skills. The dominance of English in the administrative world is still prelevent and therefore we have to focus our attention on conversation in English in India. So, English is rightly a language of technocrats.

The difficulty of the Indians using English stems not from the use of the English idioms but their build in psyche moulded by an oriental philosophy—that English is an alien language, and it is a half-truth that even an Indian can have British accent on his tongue. At the bottom, the myths may differ, but the reason remains more or less all the same in most other Asian countries. The papers in this volume attempt to quench the disturbing debates which have been so long raging over a trivial issue that whether 'Indian English' is a mere by-product of the mainstream English language, or can we ever have our own genre and a separate identity.

The death of languages is common as the death of civilisations, living beings—and the rate of the extinguish of languages is really surprising. A UNESCO report says, several hundreds of languages in Australia and America disappeared unnoticeably during the twentieth century, and that at least another 6,000 languages in the modern times are going to decline in the twenty-first century, giving space to English, and to some extent French and Chinese. To maintain a language, language planning and fostering positive attitude are the two most important things.

Language is a semiogenic process that includes symbolic, emotive and indicative functions. Thinking animal man has to exploit language to its best to be a talking animal. Language is an expression of the man himself in words in a semiogenic process; and English as a language has multifarious facets and universal features that makes it a world language today. Its simplicity of inflexion, relatively fixed words and syntax, the quality of the intonations to express shades of meaning and moods and industriousness are chiefly responsible for its popularity.

The role of English language changed in the post-Independent period as a means of social and cultural organiser. Still, a majority of English teachers still continue to work in isolation till date without realising the diverse phenomenal qualitative and quantitative growth of the language. In a state of academic confusion and dismay in the last five decades they have been shifting the language teaching approaches and course contents designing the syllabi in different ways either imported or imposed on them. At present, the second language strategies are being shifted to structural English and communicative English, separating language teaching from literature, splitting the English classics unnaturally, reducing literature and language to objective by comprehension in the name of so-called 'skills'. Still there is something praiseworthy in the Indian syllabi of English where efforts are being made to streamline teaching of literature and languages making the classrooms of English diverse in terms of space, standard, quality and approaches. The students join English as well as Spoken English courses for varied purposes—to enhance their social status, for better mobility, to prepare for competitive examinations, for dynamism in the technical world, and a very few to enter the world of literary sensibility, to study English literature as the core subject. With a view to reaching out to the different parts of the world and becoming global, now English has developed a variety of forms, each one correct within its own context, classified as national, regional, social, occupational, which is now termed as ESP, English for Specific Purposes.

The liberal educational facilities granted to the Indian teachers and students facilitate them to follow both British as well as American English as far as Communicative English is concerned. Indian bureaucrats, advertisers, technocrats, businessmen, top executives, teachers and students, as well as creative writers follow both English and American idioms and accent. Sometimes even the standard Indian textbooks follow both for potential improvement in the standards of teaching. Anyway, till date all the linguistic aspects of Indian English have not been recorded. Here, I would like to pick certain phrases, idioms, lexis, grammar, usage and pronunciation that the Indians use following both American and British English without giving a heed to the origin of these:

British English	*American English*
Ironmongery	Hardware
Carrier bag	Shopping bag
Dialling code	Area code
Engaged	Busy
Biscuit	Cookies
Flat	Apartment
Maths	Math
Plait	Braid
Rubber	Eraser
Queue	Line
Market	Mart
Aerial	Antenna
Paraffin	Kerosene
Tranquillity.	Tranquility
Jewellery	Jewelry
All right	Alright

Indian adaptability is flexible enough to accept whatever is convenient. A large-scale survey of Indian variety of English pronunciation makes it clear how the mother tongue influence works on the common mass in India. Most Bengalis and Oriyas pronounce 'sit', 'seat', 'sheet' and 'shit' alike. Malayalees' pronounce /b/ in place of /p/ in 'temple'. Most Telugus add an extra /u/ at the end or the length of vowel / a/ increases in their tongues. I have heard a fellow colleague calling Prasad, our electrician as 'Prasaadu'. Similarly, native words like 'roti', 'chapatti', 'biri', 'vilayat', 'hakim', 'basti', 'bibiji', 'harijan', 'namaskar', 'pahalwanji', etc., are being accepted by most Indian English speakers. Similarly, compound words like 'lathi-charge', 'double-roti' have one Indian and one English element in those. Thus, as far as pronunciation of English by Indians goes we cannot deny the fact that Indian variety of English is totally different from British English, still we have to accept and make improvements upon it. It is creative and resourceful, it is our socio-linguistic reality.

If we follow the words of Francis Bacon, who feels, "Reading makes a good man, conference a ready man, writing an exact man," then it must be granted that to acquire perfect writing skills is difficult as well as rewarding. Writing to learn, through observing, discovering, expressing, remembering, and investigating is central to the sequence of purposes to a good piece of writing. To promote learning, the three important sources of feelings, idea and information necessarily are explaining, evaluating and problem solving. The age-old myth that good writers are born, not made, speaks that writing is born from inspiration. All writing, even technical or business writing, is creative. Deciding what to write, how to get the reader's attention, and how to persuade your reader requires creativity and imagination.

The writing courses that many colleges and universities conduct teach how to exploit new ideas, learning concepts and processes, communicating with others, finding fresh or creative solutions to problems, or to adapt one's writing to a variety of different purposes and audiences. There are three important sources for learning, writing and communication:

investigating knowledge in books and other people, remembering and drawing on one's own experiences, observing and describing the world around.

Writing as a means of learning and communicating, begins with what we see and experience, and then connects with what we read in texts, hear in lectures or learning from the environment. The thesis, claim, or main idea in a piece of writing is related to the purpose that serves as a guide while one gathers ideas about the subject. As we collect and record information, impressions and ideas, the subject is narrowed, and the purpose is brought into sharper focus. The thesis is the dominant idea, explanation, evaluation or recommendation that we want to impress upon. Processes for writing vary form writer to writer and one writing situation to the next, but most writers identify four basic dimensions for the writing process: collecting, shaping, drafting and revising. In an age of multimedia, a writer may take the help of a computer for perfect drafting by using certain menu:

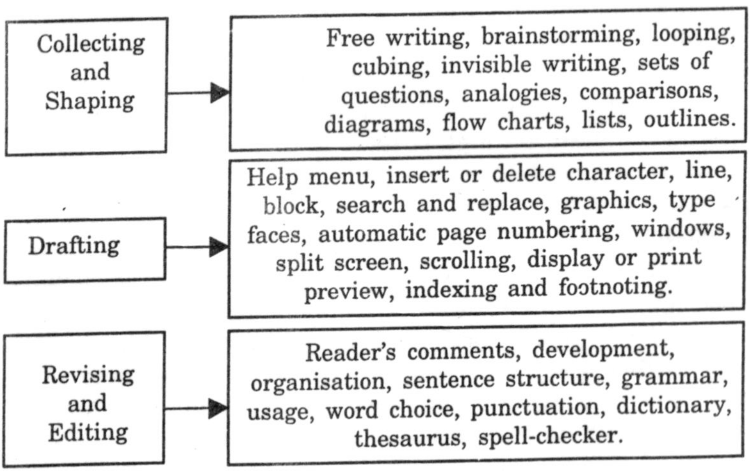

We may use any number of aids for good writing, but observation is the keyword. Whether we are writing classics, or writing in a journal, doing a laboratory report for a science class, dashing off a memo at work, writing a letter to the editor, writing on the blackboard in the classroom, keen observation is essential.

After a thorough survey of communicative skills and writing skills, I would like to move on to interpersonal skills. Our sense of identity comes from the way we relate ourselves to others and interact with them. Others define us through our behaviour and attitudes. Poor social and personal communication can contribute to coronary disease. Socially isolated people are two to three times more likely to die prematurely than those with strong social ties. Divorced men die of strokes, ailments and cancer at double rate of married men. The rate of suicide among them is five times more than married persons. A variety of other needs like safety, protection, personal development, progress, self-esteem, accomplishments and a sense of sharing are fulfilled through communication and relationships. A person's self-concept or self-image is known to affect his communication ability. The way we feel about ourselves has a direct bearing on how we communicate with others. The differences in the behavioral patterns have been brought out in a variety of research. The most significant part of a person's self-concept might consist of social roles. For another it might be physical appearance, friendships, community service or accomplishments.

Psychologists emphasize on the need to recognise the existence of three selves that each individual possesses: The perceived self—the person we know we are in private moments of total honesty; the presenting self—the image we project or the face we show to the world; the desired self—the way we would like to be the ideal person we wish to become. When an individual maintains a balance between all the three, he may be successful.

1

Changing Contours of Communication:

Some Effects of Modern Science and Technologies on English Language and Literature

M.L.Das

PROLOGUE

Before we enter into a comparatively serious discussion on language, communication and technical education kindly permit me tell you two small anecdotes which may elucidate the importance of language: the one is related to one of the African languages and the other to French. A British Member of Parliament, Hugh Dykes, once narrated the first story. A senior politician, once, was on an official visit of one of the newly independent African republics, and on landing at a remote rural airstrip, he was invited by the chiefs to address the assembled natives. He went through the usual ritual phrases – "marvellous to be here" "Wonderful country", "Challenge of independence", and was happy to note that, at the end of each sentence and paragraph of his oration, the enthusiastic natives shouted out, "Umbula, Umbula."

He concluded his speech to yet more outbursts of "Umbula, Umbula", and was then driven away to inspect a new farm.

As he was going through the cattle pens with the farm manager, he was very dismayed when the manager said to him, "Be careful where you step, there is a lot of Umbula about from the cows."

The second anecdote is about an English tourist's experience in France and was told by Lord Aberdare.

An English tourist, who rather fancied his meagre knowledge of French, went over on a day trip to Calais and had a meal in a restaurant. He found a fly in his soup and summoned the waiter by calling out a very Anglicised version of 'Garcon'. When the waiter arrived, he pointed at the fly floating in the soup and said repeatedly "le mouch, le mouch"! The waiter with great dignity replied, "Excusez moi, Monsieur. Clest la mouche!" "Good heavens"! said the diner, "I must say, you Frenchmen have marvellous eyesight."

Ignorance of language may put you in ridiculous to dangerous situations. Doesn't that speak of the importance of language?

The very theme of the present workshop reverberates a profound sincerity of purpose on the part of the institution : you are trying to find out the worth and degree of utility of the subjects that you propose to teach to your students. What to teach, how much to teach and how to teach are the questions that come to the minds of genuine planners and executors of education. The present workshop is intended to weigh and measure the importance of language studies in technical education (of course not with the Satirical undertone of the Hindi film song "hamare angana me tumhara kya kaam hai?"). One of the two objectives of this workshop as enunciated in the preamble passage of the circulated brochure aims at "an analysis of the fact why language studies are highly required in technical education", which in itself entails the questions about the nature, shape and quantum of language studies in engineering colleges. Perhaps we need to have a clearly identified and succinctly defined policy of language studies for the students of science and technology and, then, we also need to reorient the curriculum to be followed.

Policy of Language Teaching in Technical Colleges

The policy of language studies for technical education will largely depend on the objectives of, and, expectations from technical education. The objectives of technical education are more or less the same as those of general higher education. The tasks of universities and other institutions of higher learning are no longer confined to two traditional functions of teaching and advancement of knowledge. They are assuming new functions, and the older ones are increasing in range, depth and complexity. In broad terms they are expected:

a) to seek and cultivate new knowledge, to engage vigorously and fearlessly in the pursuit of truth, and to interpret old knowledge and beliefs in the light of new needs and discoveries;

b) to provide the right kind of leadership in all walks of life, to identify gifted youth and to help them develop their potential to the full;

c) to provide society with competent men and women trained in agriculture, arts, medicine, science and technology and various other professions, who will also be cultivated individuals, imbued with a sense of social purpose;

d) to strive to promote all-round development; and

e) to foster in teachers and students, and through them in society generally, the attitudes and values needed for developing the 'good life' in individuals and society.

(Education Commission, 1966, pp.274-75)

A student coming out of engineering colleges will become a professional technocrat or a researcher engaged on expanding the horizons of human knowledge, but it is perhaps more important or at least equally important for him to spread technical or scientific learning or knowledge among the people of his society and country. He is expected to master a means of communication which will enable him to gather knowledge new and old, from books and journals published all over the world in English. He therefore must master the English language which has become widely respected as a language of culture, commerce and all kinds of international communication. With this objective of acquiring world-wide technical knowledge. you teach English in technical institutions (how do you do it is a subject which I will refer to later in this paper). The professional technocrat has also to scatter scientific awareness, to spread the knowledge of science and technology among his countrymen, and for this purpose he must master an Indian language, preferably the national language, Hindi. If you are recommending any language policy for technical education at this workshop I will earnestly request you to weigh in the two-language policy for technical and scientific education.

Communication, Language and Education

But perhaps I have digressed, perhaps I am guilty of counting chickens before locating the eggs. The theme of this workshop is: "the importance of language studies...", etc., which is related with more basic questions, like, what is language and what are its functions? The simplest answer is that language is a means of communication which is one of the basic and essential requirements of man. Communication is the interplay of man's relationship in his endeavour to understand the world and the self. Its goal is communion. Whether through gestures, signals, music, paintings, dances or languages, human communication is a complex and varied affair. In its simplest meaning, communication is a means of giving and receiving information, feelings, emotions and thoughts, a means of acquiring and disseminating intelligence and knowledge. And this communication is the primary and ultimate business of language which, spoken or written, man invented for the transportation of ideas and experiences.

In other words language is a great machine tool which makes human culture possible, which, more obviously than anything else, distinguishes man from the rest of the animal world. It is an affair of a group. It has multiplicity of functions, the basic one of which is that it enables us to influence people's behaviour. To be brief, "a language is a signalling system which operates with symbolic vocal sounds and which is used by some groups of people for the purposes of communication and social co-operation. (C.L. Barber, *The Story of Language*, p.26).

It is indeed very interesting to note that the emergence of language was the outcome of countless, nameless revolutions that went with the onward march of civilisations. Communication in the beginning was a matter of signs and gestures, then came sounds (spoken speech), then the hieroglyphs, ideograms, then the rules of grammar were made. Language (spoken) underwent countless changes since it arose, and it took thousands and thousands of years for man to develop language as a suitable vehicle for transporting what he felt or thought, dreamt or discovered, experienced and stored as knowledge to be disseminated, It continues to grow, evolve and change adopting to the material needs of users, and taking new shapes under the impact of every technological revolution. The dissemination of stored language is the basis and meaning of education.

Education, whether technical, liberal, philosophical, spiritual or otherwise is also a group affair demanding flow of information, experience and knowledge from the giver to receiver, from the 'guru' to the pupil. Written language changed drastically the nature of learning and created a new definition of education. Had there been no written language, knowledge, at best would have remained a matter of memory and would have been lost. The living wisdom of the community, as embodied in memory, began to yield to written and dated papers as a standard of truth; every important event or transaction was recorded. And these records have remained as the unfathomable and deathless treasures of human knowledge and education. No education can be imparted in a vacuum in the absence of a language.

In the discussions that follow we will restrict the meaning of 'education' to technical education and of 'language' to English language, not withstanding the fact that I have recommended adoption of a two-language (English + Hindi) policy for institutions of technology.

Impact of Social and Technological Changes

Language has been an ever-growing ever-changing phenomenon, changing under the impact of social and technological changes and the users of language have always been adapting to the effective, optimum use of language, be it with the help of language laboratories or learning in the classrooms or trying it in different kinds of media.

The English language has changed considerably in the last thousand years. New words have appeared, and some old ones disappeared. Words have changed in meaning. The grammatical endings of words have changed. There have been changes in word order, in the ways in which words can be arranged to make meaningful utterances. Pronunciation has changed. Taken all together these changes add up to a major transformation of language.

There have been many reasons causing changes in grammar syntax, vocabulary and pronunciation. We have no time and space to discuss all the reasons for linguistic changes. But one reason that we cannot fail to take notice of is the various kinds of technological change that have necessitated linguistic changes.

We can identify two kinds of technological change. One, let us do the same things more quickly and cheaply. The other leads us to different things and perhaps even to become in some way different people. The revolution in spinning and weaving technology around A.D., 1800 for example, brought great economic change in Europe and North America but did not bring a comparable social revolution. On the other hand, rail, road, airplane networks did affect profoundly our notions of time, distance and travel, and brought structural changes in commercial and residential use of space. Telegraph services and typewriters made business communications more efficient; telephones brought new kinds of interactions, not simply greater speed. In the twentieth century the advent of space, exploration, technologies and satellites, the coming of computers, cybernetics and other microelectronic devices have revolutionised and almost changed human civilisation and its communication systems. The recent technological transformation ushering in a new "information society" has introduced "cyberpunk" and "Cyborg" and an endless variety of concepts the communication of which expressly demands a new handling of language.

This has happened earlier almost in all ages that new concepts, new discoveries, new outlooks have demanded new vistas of expression with new words, new structures and new styles. By about A.D. 1700 English spellings and pronunciations were nearly standardised. The pronouns "thou" and "thee" and the corresponding verb forms like "lovest" had disappeared from everyday educated use.

The seventeenth century saw the triumph of scientific outlook in England and science has had a pervasive influence on the language and the way it has been used during the past three hundred years. Latin gave way to English as the language of science and scholarship. The rise of scientific writing in English helped to establish a simple referential kind of prose. The plain style became popular.

Strong support for the plain style came from the scientists during this century. It was an age that saw a marked growth in scientific curiosity and the scientific attitude of mind. Many advances were made in man's knowledge of the universe. Early in the century, William Harvey discovered circulation of the blood and, later, Isaac Newton discovered the laws of motion and principle of gravity. Francis Bacon advocated a scientific and rational approach to the world, while Thomas Hobbes adopted a scientific attitude to the study of politics and psychology. They wanted to keep words as close as possible to real things. They preferred plain glass to coloured glass because it let through more light.

The development of science was marked by the foundation of the Royal Society in 1660. This society aimed at encouraging experiments and discouraged extravagance and fine writing in the reports of the Society. Science in the seventeenth century showed an altogether new handling of language.

In 1667 Thomas Sprat wrote a history of the Royal Society, the already mentioned first scientific society in England, and the most famous till this day. In this book he made an attack on rhetorical and figurative language.

> [There has been] a constant Resolution to reject all amplifications, digressions, and swellings of style: to return back to the primitive purity, and shortness, when men delivered so many things, almost in equal number of words. They have exacted from all their members, a close, naked, natural way of speaking; positive expressions; clear senses; a native easiness; bringing all things as near the Mathematical plainness as they can: and preferring the language of artisans, countrymen, and merchants, before that of wits or scholars.

This passage shows clearly that the Royal Society and the scientists of the seventeenth century exercised a significant influence on the language of the time, pronouncing the idea that language should be plainly expressive and close to real things.

The scientific and technological advancements also make a major contribution towards enriching the language by bringing in a flood of new words produced by the scientific necessities. The sixteenth century had introduced especially words to do with the human body, like *skeleton, tibia, abdomen,* and *tendon* and also a number of diseases like *catarrh, epilepsy, mumps and smallpox*. In seventeenth century too, the new scientific words were predominantly medical and biological (*vertebra, tonsil, pneumonia, lumbago*); but there were also quite a few new words in chemistry (including *acid*), in physics (including *atmosphere, equilibrium* and *gravity*) and in mathematics (including *formula, logarithm* and *series*). In the eighteenth century came enormous expansion in the vocabulary of biological sciences, for this was the great age of biological description and classification. From this period came many of the descriptive terms of zoology and botany, like *albino, coleoptera, anther, fauna, dicotyledon, habitat, pistil* and so on. The great changes in chemical theory in the late eighteenth century also produced many new words including *hydrogen, oxygen nitrogen* and *molecule*.

In the nineteenth century, the expansion became explosive; many specialised scientific fields were developing fast and though many of the scientific new words have never had large public use, many flooded the common use like *accumulator, dynamo, cereal, hibernate, pasteurised, conifer, ozone* and *metabolism*, etc. In the twentieth century science and technology went nuclear, rose to the unimaginable heights in space and rode on the electronic waves or wonders. Nuclear physics had a very deep effect on human civilisation, changing our conception of the universe and also creating the possibilities for extermination. The new words that got made are countless, but some that are in the common parlance are words like *proton, neutron, electron, reactor, radioactive* and *isotope*. In the world of medicine, words like *vitamin, penicillin, antibiotic* came in. Words like *stratosphere, supersonic, nylon, transistor, television, electronic* are some of the products of the twentieth century scientific and technological advancements.

I have already mentioned how the recent technological transformations bring in a new space and information society, with its endless variety of new concepts. This has further necessitated a major change in the handling of language.

Engineers, technologists and scientists have the challenge of making a vehicle for communicating efficiently, and with ease and plainness, the new concepts and ideas of a new era. Linguists in general and the teachers and students of engineering colleges have new grounds to tread in preparing human resources to carry on the burden of ever-expanding new knowledge of the twenty-first century.

The Twenty-First Century: Language and Technology

The twenty-first century man, riding the crest of great technological and scientific advancements, has started experiencing formidable changes in the means and modes of communication. This phenomenon has been variously described as microelectronic or the communication or information revolution. Its impact on the society has been regarded as analogus to the impact the railways had on the mid-nineteenth century. As a matter of fact all technological changes affect the style and shape of life in societies. These also influence the courses of communication which ultimately stamp their effects on language and literature.

Alvin Toffler, in his book *The Third Waev*, views microelectronics technology or information technology, to have a potentiality to affect society comparable to the industrial revolution. Aldous Huxley, in his book *Literature and Science*, published around 1962, tried to discern ways in which literary artists might come to grips with accelerating scientific and technological revolution. Huxley observed that his contemporaries, though gravely concerned with "the social and psychological consequences of advancing technology," have been very little interested in technology itself. He viewed the difficulties inherent in wedding science to literature as a challenge of intellectual combat. About two decades later than Aldous Huxley's reflections on the relationship of science and literature, Tracy Kidder, in her book, *The Soul of a New Machine*, described building a super mini-computer and in its pages engineer Tom West and the whizkids who built it, show all the creativity and intensity of purpose.

In *The SOul of a New Machine* Tracy Kidder provides a factual accounting of how, between mid-1978 and early 1980, a group of engineers, at Data General Corporation, developed a new super mini-computer. Anyone interested in the annals of American industry will find the story absorbing. Kidder, a freelance journalist and the author of *The Road to Yuba City*, has endowed the tale with such pace, texture and poetic implication that she has elevated it to a high level of narrative art. The machine has made a good story, the contents of science and technology imitate the run of human life and, framed in a suitable language, make a piece of enjoyable literature. The challenge of wedding science to literature is surmounted. This has been done for quite sometime now, particularly in science fiction. We now see centres of higher learning using computers in studying literature. Classics scholars at Princeton University study Virgil with the help of computer programmes to scan the text quickly, picking out passages that contain the same words used in different contexts. This reduces the drudgery, they claim, and allows them more time to study meaning. Dartmouth applies similar analytical techniques to the *Bible* and Shakespeare. Apparently, students are integrating the technology into their academic lives as easily as they did the simple calculator a couple of decades ago.

In brief, science and technology have influenced the generation of a significant section of English literature in our times.

More than they have influenced literature, science and technologies have affected English language, particularly during the last 40 years or so of the twentieth century. The twenty-first century continues to use its chisels, sculpting new faces and figures of English language. Computers and microelectronics devices including mobile phones and websites have affected the English structures, syntax, lexicon and styles of expressions. Around the time Aldous Huxley published his book *Literature and Science*, a new era in Western society was ushered in by computers and space technologies and to underpin that new era the vocabulary went through some changes. The new technologies, like the seventeenth century sciences, generated endlessly new terms. New terms got minted which entered the new vocabulary. Science, which *inter alia*, can claim the longest word in the English language—the proper chemical name of 'tryptophan synthetase A Protein' – a 1913 letter enzyme with 267 amino acids leads the field in such creativity. (I am sorry I can't remember the word to tell you.) Computing, another linguistic gusher, is similarly productive of new terms. The first business machines appeared in the early 1950's, and as they developed they accrued much of the vocabulary that has become commonplace today. The personal computer revolution of the 1980's have brought new storms in the sea of English vocabulary. The meaning of the word "language" itself has assumed new dimensions; it no longer stands only for English, Latin, Greek, German, French, Sanskrit Hindi, etc., it stands for newer languages, that is BASIC (1966, an acronym for Beginners' All Purpose Symbolic Instruction), or LOGO or COBOL (1970, an acronym for Common Business-Oriented Language), Forth (1969, a programming language for fourth generation computers).

And there emerged "programming languages" necessary to operate computers. Words like "Floppy disc", "Laptop, "windows", "Workstation", "GIGO", etc., are some samples of new coinages. There are some comparatively difficult terms like OOP (Object Oriented Processing) and GUI (Graphical User Interface) which are increasingly becoming wellknown as more and more people use computing machines.

Not only the new vocabulary, the computers are developing new textures of language, sometimes terse and tiring for old teachers and students. A reader who wishes to unravel a paragraph such as this (I quote):

> The I/O registers pertain predominantly to the XGA's display controller. The memory-mapped registers, however, refer primarily to the graphics co-processor. The XGA's power-on self-test routines set the base addresses for both registers.

will have to curse a teacher like me and to look elsewhere. There is no doubt that the machines are forcing new languages or old language in new attires. If you and I don't learn them we will be fossilised. Institutions therefore, may adapt CALL (Computer Aided Languages Learning).

One of the peculiar characteristics of language learning has been the principle of minimum effort in maximum communication. It is this weakness for minimum effort that makes you call ND for Dr. Nandini Sahu or IDNP for Dr. Dr. I.D.N.Prasad or 'math' or 'bio' for mathematics and biology. Linguists have used this method earlier to shorten words and coin new words.

Thus cabriolet became 'cab' photograph—'photo'; public house—'pub'; permanent wave —'perm'; 'aeroplane'—'plane'; 'brassiere'—'bra'; television—'telly', and the like. But in the twenty-first century mobile phones, e-mail and website facilites have not only retained this shortening tendency faster than ever, but have made the language also digital. Perhaps a modern-day Julius Caesar would not like to exclaim "Et Tu Brute = you too Brutus", but he may only write electronically "U2Bru". My son once sent me a SMS question: "R U Coming B4Mom"? and my experience of teaching English language and literature for more than 40 years reeled in dismay. But this is the way the world is changing; language is changing, if you don't catch up, you fail and vanish out of scene.

When communication was between man and man or man and animal, language had its traditional (developed over centuries) shape, size and sensitivity. Now communications have forced transportation of knowledge between man and machine, and between machine and machine. This takes us to new dimensions and directions, and students and teachers of languages must prepare themselves to tread on new grounds which this workshop may identify.

Perhaps there is a greater need to learn and master the new era language, more for the technocrats than the general people. The students of science and technology have to acquire the latest knowledge that computers, electronics, space-avionics and other branches deal in. Chinese and Russians are facing great difficulties in capturing the world market, despite their being new leaders in many technologies, because they are not well versed in English. You should not be amazed at the Chinese learning English even in New Zealand. They have to compete, live in the race and ride on the horses of world language.

The importance of language studies in technical education need not be highlighted any further. Opting for technical education without mastering English language will be like jumping from an aeroplane without a parachute. But as I said, if you want to be a successful technologist or technocrat within your country and if you wish to benefit your countrymen by spreading facts and attitudes of science and technology, you must earn the felicity of communicating in your national language, Hindi.

I am not sure if I have communicated my ideas to you well. I should like to close my talk by telling, again, a small anecdote.

A 16-year-old reporter for *Childrens Express*, a newspaper published then, entirely by school children, characterised *The Fourth Assembly of the World*, in July 1982, whose theme was the new world of telecommunications, said:

"I think the message was clear that it is really our (young people's) world. I was kind of laughing at the people here. This technology, all they talked about, they really couldn't grasp. This belongs to us."

The computer-electronics-generated language belongs to the younger generation, whether they laugh or we laugh is not going to sweep off the message. Languages and other means of communication will keep changing making it convenient to carry the new burdens of knowledge.

2

Making Core Subjects More Communicative

B.B.Badhai

Communicative method of teaching presupposes a graded pattern of imparting academics so as to make it learner-friendly. Language being the extant and common medium, communicative method of teaching aims at simplifying things at the linguistic level so as to make things coherent. Further, cogency of thought and expression is achieved through various interactive methods of putting the content in order to acquaint the learner with the basics. It is now commonly accepted that the chalk and talk method is a failure in the technology-savvy scenario that we as teachers are put into. Hence, teaching as a method must also accommodate the change and reshuffle its fundamentals to suit the needs. Here, I would like to highlight the necessity of making the core subjects adhere to the patterns of communicative method of teaching. Communicative method of teaching (CMT) involves an interctive method, with emphasis on activity-oriented learning instead of teaching as a sort of preaching from a high pedestal.

All the subjects are aimed at the learners. Here the teachers / authors of books are the medium through which subjects reach the learners. But the subjects in their content are not much communicative so that the learners shall be able to understand the subjects by themselves. In between the subject and the learner there may be a teacher who facilitates the process of learning. Thus, we cannot ignore the third element, i.e., the teacher's role in facilitating as it is the teacher who understands the subject matter, gathers information and gives shape to his thought to bring it into a communicative fold and ultimately delivers them to the learners. The method should be to gradually expose the learners to the nuances of a subject instead of being forcefully thrust into it, which very often results in making the learners lose interest for the subject.

The shaping or designing the message depends upon the strength, weakness, likeness, disliking, etc., of the teachers and the students. The capacity of the teacher to understand the students and their needs play a major role in shaping the message. Apart from that, the proficiency of shaping the message in appropriate form is an important task in itself. Sometimes the teachers understand the subject matter perfectly but fail to give a proper shape to their thought to be transferred to the learners effectively. Such shaping of thought will differ from person to person which is the primary thing responsible for the variance in the art of making the students understand the subject matter. Many individuals might know the same thing and the sources of their information may be the same, yet when expessing, their recipients may vastly differ in their understanding. The major reason behind such a variation may be the variation in their level of communication skills.

It is seen that the teachers who are more communicative are well accepted and become more popular with the students in comparison to the teachers possessing low level of communication skills. Teachers with good communication skills shall be able to grasp the difficulties of the students and may design their explanations best suited to the occasion using appropriate examples.

A subject is never easy or difficult. It is the persons who due to their inefficiency, have complicated it. No subject is born difficult. It is we who have made a subject easy or difficult and classified it accordingly. It is the so-called experts who have sown the seeds of fear in the mind of the learners due to which they perceive a subject as difficult. A subject is difficult only because we have not been able to simplify it. If we know it, it is easy, if we don't, it is difficult. A subject may be difficult for one but may be easy for another. So here the problem lies not with the subject but with the learner and the teacher. Only a systematic approach shall be helpful to convert the difficult into the easy.

Nowadays the role of a teacher in teaching has come down, and the level of dependence of the students on the teacher has also been reduced drastically. Such a situation is happy and sad at the same time. It is happy if the situation is the result of the learner's self-dependence and sad if we become incomprehensive and unrealiable to them. effectiveness of the teacher cannot be assured and can never be stadardised. There shall be variation in the standards of teaching and ultimately the standard of learning. Here, there is the need of making subjects more communicative by emphasizing on learning rather than on teaching. This is probably due to the increase in the communitiveness of the subjects through books. Under this textbooks may contain topics/chapters which are more interactive and activity oriented. There may be the extensive use of pictures, models, charts, examples, tasks, descriptions, etc., involving the learners. Efforts may be made to redesign the subjects / chapters in such a manner that they are interactive in nature or be self-communicative where the teachers may simply act as a guide to the students focusing on learners only which will make the learner self-dependent and confident about the subject.

Here, I would like to take an opportunity to demonstrate with an example. Mostly when we are teaching writing skill we often move from the theory to the examples and then on to practise. But reversing the process may have a still better result. Suppose I am assigned the task of teaching paragraph writing to the students. Instead of giving theories of paragraph writing I may start the process of giving them a complete paragraph of the type I am to teach. Here, the student may try to familiarise himself to the content rather than imagining it. After that the student may be given some example and so on. Here, the communicative method of teaching attracts concrete association of the learner in the process.

In the process, I would like to point out some valuable suggestion to have a small beginning to make the core subjects more communicative:

1) All the teachers and writers of books should be made to improve their communication skills by increasing the language input in them so as to use them in transferring learning.
2) All the textbooks should be collaborative and must associate at least a language expert to simplify the expression to make it attractive, interesting and learner-friendly. They may suggest suitable substitute / alternative words and expression to the contents.
3) Subject vocabulary should be made compulsory at the end of each chapter of the book so as to enable the learners to understand the subject matter without the help of experts. Meanings of different words and expressions used in the text must be explained in detail for better understanding.
4) The textbooks may be rewritten to accommodate the extensive use of pictures, tables, flowcharts, models, examples, etc., and make the content interactive as well as activity-oriented.
5) The criteria for selection of teachers and authors should be based on the communicative skill apart from their resourcefulness.
6) Communicative language studies should be open to all subject experts.
7) At the higher level of studies, curriculum should include some exercises by the learners to make the chapters / topics / expressions more simplified. The teaching of simplification procedures may make the subjects more communicative.
8) To make the core subjects like physics, chemistry, mathematics, botany, zoology, bio-technology, civil,

electrical, etc., more communicative efforts may be made by the academicians to simplify the useful portion of the subjects for easy communication among the masses.

I understand that such an activity may look difficult presently but a good beginning shall show the light to overcome the difficulties.

The real purpose of education is to transfer the knowledge to the masses, and the purpose of academics is to transfer it perfectly. Hence to make the subjects more communicative the focus should be on the teachers so that they are able to develop / design the topics / chapters / subjects in an interactive manner. We should remember that a teacher is more for the sub-standard and average students rather than for the good students. A teacher is supposed to be an expert so far as the content of the subject is concerned but may not be an expert in language which is the vessel of communication. So he has to be a good navigator to guide the vessel to the shores. Unless he has a good command over the language, he may be a handicap and fail to give appropriate shape to the messages and thought for transmission. He may be resourceful but may not be tactful enough in the art of communication.

3

Generative Phonology and Post-generative Scenario

Gobardhan Sahu

The present article aims at analysing the implication of generative phonology and tries to make a brief survey of the post-generative scenario. It is presumed that the inherent principles of the Chomskian generative phonology will be of immense help in the acquistion of a foreign language like English by the Indian learners.

As a matter of fact, the sole function of sound in language is to keep utterances apart. The phonological system of a language is, therefore, not so much "a set of sounds" as it is a "network of differences between sounds." A particular speech sound, though in terms of articulation is the same, it is not exactly the same in terms of acoustic or auditory qualities. For example, English /p/ will have different qualities depending upon who the speaker is. The perception of /p/ is an utterance (depending upon what his mother tongue has taught him), the person who hears it, the medium through which it is spoken (telephone or television or radio), the environment in which it is spoken (total silence or total noise). That is why we prefer to talk in terms of phonemes—not phones—and say that English /p/ is a phoneme.

A phoneme is, therefore, difined as the smallest contrastive unit in the sound system of a language. The phonemes of a language, then, are the elements which stand in contrast with each other in the phonological system of the language. In all phonological analysis it is necessary to recognise both phonetic units (phones) and phonological units (phonemes). All phonologists agree on the basic units and phonological units. But beyond this basic point of agreement they differ on the nature of the phoneme.

The first formulation of phonomic theory is mostly ascribed to Jan Baudouin de Courtenay, an eminent Polish linguist. Soon after, Henry Sweet, Paul Passey and Danil Jones enquired into the nature of phoneme. More or less, they believed in the following few salient features of phonemes:

i) Phonemes are language-specific and unique.

ii) Phonemes are groups of similar sounds—each phoneme being a family of sounds—which are closely related to each other.

iii) Phonemes have positional variants called "allophones" which are in complementary distribution.

iv) Phonemes bring about distinctions in meaning because they are the minimal distinctive sound segments of a language.

v) Phonemes are generally symmentrical in nature.

As a strong reaction against the above phonemic principle, J.R.Firth propounded the prosodic analysis of language. It explicitly recognised the features that may be called "non-segmental". These features, otherwise called prosodies fall in there groups: (i) Demarcative prosodies (ii) Prosodies characteristic of the longer features, and (iii) Morphological prosodies. Demarcative prosodies are, in fact, not realised over a whole or a large part of a structure. However, they serve the purpose of delimiting it, for instance, "aspiration" to mark initial syllable in some situations in English. Prosodies characteristic of the longer piece, are related with a syllable, a word, a phrase or a sentence. Morphological prosodies link grammar with phonetics.

Trubetzkoy, Jakobson and other members of the Prague School of Linguistics also challenge the phonemic analysis. They claim that a phoneme could be further analysable into distinctive features. To put Giegerich's words, "While a phoneme cannot by definition be broken up into shorter successive units, it can be viewed as a bundle of simultaneous units called phonological features: individual properties whose sum makes up the phoneme (1994:89). The English phoneme /b/, for example, is regarded as a bundle of features [+ labial - alveolar + voiced - strident - continuant]. These bundles of features distinguish /b/ from /p/ which is [+bilabial - alveolar - voiced - strident - continuant]. Description in terms of features helps us draw relations not only between sounds, but also between the sound systems of different languages. Generative phonology makes use of distinctive features for analysing a language as they are considered to be the ultimate building blocks of phonology.

The publication of Chomsky and Halle's *The Sound Pattern of English* (1968) marked the emergence of generative phonology as a new theory and framework for the analysis of languages. Those who belonged to this new school of linguists, that is, the Transformational Generativists, were critical of the structuralists' approach current during that time. Chomsky himself accused them of attaching undue concern with inventories of elements and a classificatory approach to linguistic analysis. Instead, the generativisits held that linguistic description ought to aim at constructing a grammar that would generate linguistic forms. The phonological component of such a grammar would be a set of phonological rules applying to the underlying forms of the language yielding surface phonetic representations. Since both underlying and surface forms were represented in features, the rules essentially changed features, specifications and the shape of a phonological description and was indeed radically different from a typical inventory of phonemes and allophones.

Chomsky's *The Sound Pattern of English* is based to a great extent on Jakobson, Fant and Halle (1952) and Jakobson and Halle (1956). But it offers several modifications and improves upon the earlier two works. These modifications are related with the specific set of distinctive features used to capture contrasts and conceptualisation of these features. They are designed to capture the phonological contrasts of language and to describe the phonetic content of segments derived by phonological rules. The 1952 and the 1956 Jakobsonian models of distinctive features started the features in terms of their acoustic characteristics. However, in the SPE model, in 1968, Chomsky and Halle modified the previous model, where the features were redefined and restated in terms of their articulatory characteristics. In other words, sounds were described in terms of how they were produced in the vocal tract cavity. Chomsky and Halle envisaged 27 features to capture phonological contrasts of language. They divided the features in to major class features, cavity features, manner of articulation features as source features. Further, they listed prosodic features, though did not discuss them in detail:

Major Class Features	:	Sonorant, Vocalic, Consonantal
Cavity Features	:	Coronal, Anterior, High, Low, Back, Round, Distributed, Covered, Glottal contriction, Nasal, Lateral.
Mannerof Articulation Features	:	Continuant, Instantaneous release, Velaric suction, Implosion, Velaric pressure, Ejection, Tense.
Source Features	:	Stress, Pitch, Length.

The distinctive features as used in generative phonology are characterised by three main tendencies as explained in the following lines:

a) The tendency to establish a relatively small set of distinctive features for the analysis of the phonological structures of all languages. It aims to be a part of a universal phonetic theory which needs formulation of universal constraints on feature co-occurrence and feature contrasts.

b) The tendency to interpret phonetic correlates of distinctive features not in articulatary terms alone but in terms of categories which can be given an acoustic as well as articulatory interpretation.

c) The tendency to interpret all possible contrasts or similarities in terms of one or several binary features, having '+' or '-' values.

The basic goal of generative phonology is to account for all the linguistically significant sounds produced by the human vocal apparatus. For this purpose, two levels of representations are used in generative phonology, viz., 'Systematic phonemic representation' and 'Systematic phonetic representation'. The systematic phonemic representation is an underlying phonological representation, an utterance which is converted into the systematic phonetic, one by a set of rules called phonological rules or P-rules. Morphemes are represented at the systematic phonetic level by a sequencee of columns containing the required distinctive features specifications. Each column represents a segment, the concern here being the features within segments rather than with segments as a whole.

At the systematic phonetic level, utterances are made up of morphemes and junctures which are related to feature columns, corresponding to the phones of a traditional segmental description. The feature matrices at the systematic phonetic level differs from those at the phonemic level in that they are fully specified for all classificatory features, and the features themselves have numerical values in addition to plus or minus values.

Phonological rules apply to sentences sequentially, and very often in a specific order. Each application of the P-rule brings about a change in the phonological representation of the sentence in some way or another, leading to the final phonetic representation. Most generative phonologists frequently quote rules containing segmental symbols. A sequence of segments in comparable notation is referred to as a 'matrix', because each segment can be considered as a set of values entered against the features. The word 'peak' [PI:K] may be displayed in the following way:

P	*I*	*K*
– Syllabic	+ Syllabic	– Syllabic
+ Consonantal	– Consonantal	+ Consonantal
– Voiced	+ Voiced	– Voiced
– High	+ High	+ High
... (etc) ...	... (etc) ...	... (etc) ...

Generative phonology commanded great currency in the 1970's and the 1980's. However, it was not without its natural reactive offshoots. Some of such reactions were in the forms of Natural Generative Phonology, Natural Phonology, Autosegmental Phonology, CV Phonology, Metrical Phonology, Lexical Phonology, Dependency Phonology, and Experimental Phonology. We present below a brief discussion on the post-generative scenario.

Natural generative phonology (NGP) emerges from a few paper by Vennemann in the 1970's and is most comprehensively expounded by Hooper. The proponents describe their school as based in part on transformational generative theory as developed since the mid-1950's but point to a major difference concerning the abstractness of phonological representations and rules. In a sense, NGP directs phonology back towards the more concrete concerns of phonemics. This point is underlined by Hooper's recognition of a distinction among rules that virtually revives the traditional categorisation into phonetic and morphophonemic rules. Hooper distinguishes between rules that refer only to phonetic information and reflect the automatic pronunciation habits of a speaker.

Natural phonology originates from David Stampe's dissertation on natural phonology published in 1979. It stresses on phonological processes in the context of children's acquisition of phonology. This processes are not rules of the language but reflections of what we might call the child's inbuilt tendencies. Thus, by the nature of the human articulatory and perceptual organism, a child will prefer to articulate plosives as voiceless rather than voiced because of the relative difficulty of maintaining voicing, while the supraglottal tract is closed off or will prefer to nasalise vowels next to nasal consonant. Donegan and Stampe claim that their theory is natural because it seeks to explain why language is the way it is.

The phrase 'Auto Segmental Phonology' is the title of Goldsmith's dissertation published in 1976. His initial concern is with that of segmental organisation, or more particularly, that of phenomena which have evaded segmental classification. His thesis announces a claim about the 'geometry' of phonetic representatin in the context of what he calls 'the absolute slicing hypothesis'. It is concerned with a multilinear phonological analysis. Autosegmental phonology points out that speech consists of gestures such as tongue movement, lip movement, and laryngeal activity, which are coordinated but which by no means start and finish all at the same instant. Goldsmith himself remarks that the system of analysis itself was originally suited to fit the intricacies of Aftican tone languages.

The concept of CV phonology arose from work by Kahn on syllabic organisation. The original contribution of CV phonology is the postulation of a CV tier, a tier of C and V 'slots' which are filled by the segments. CV phonology offers the possibility of capturing the special nature of complex segments that traditionally require structural interpretaion. Thus, a diphthong can be shown as two vowel qualities functioning as, or filling the position of, a single vowel; or a lengthened or geminate consonant can be represented as a single segment spreading over two C positions.

Metrical phonology has its origin in a doctoral dissertation submitted by Liberman in 1979. It began as a theory of stress and later widened its horizons. It assumes that stress patterns reflect an underlying structure in which stronger and weaker constituents are juxtaposed. To say that a certain syllable is stressed is to make a judgment about its strength relative to adjacent syllable.

Originally developed by Strauss, Kiparsky and Mohanan, lexical phonology shows a revived interest in morphology, and asserts a level of representation, which is comparable to that of taxonomic phonemics. It does allow for abstract underlying forms and in that light is 'a standard generative phonology'. Lexical rules are fed by morphology. The morphological component supplies the various affixed and compounded forms of the language, and lexical rules then apply, to modify these froms in accordance with the phonological requirements of the language.

Dependency phonology, propounded by Anderson et al in 1985, shaves much of the modern interest in structures, such as feet and syllables and in the organisation of features below the level of the segment. It is possible to model the structural organisation of speech in a way that is reminiscent of metrical tree structures but different in important respects. There are no category symbols in dependency phonology. Structural relations are shown by dependency alone, reflected in the tree diagram. Here the vowel is most prominent, and the consonants are dependent in the analysis of a syllable.

Experimental phonology represents an attempt to draw together at least three research styles: experimental phonetics, experimental psychology and phonological thoery. This move is not always free of the implication that phonology is speculative and that evidence obtained experimentally is superior to any other kind of evidence. Proponents of experimental phonology like Ohala, Jaeger, Hombart and Campbell take a rather generous view of what constitutes an experiment, and emphasize observation and careful refinement of one's beliefs rather than reliance on instrumental investigation. Both Hombart and Campbell suggest that evidence from word games provides a test of the psychological reality of phonological rules and structures.

Thus, quite a few phonological studies came into existence which are directly or indirectly related with generative phonology as envisaged by chomsky and Halle in *The Sound Pattern of English* (1968).

References

Anderson, S.R., 1974, *The Organisation of Phonology,* New York : Seminar Press.

Chomsky, Noam, *Syntactic Structure,* The Hague: Mouton, 1957.

____________ and Morris Halle, *The Sound Pattern of English,* New York: Harper and Row, 1968.

Clark, John and Collin Yallop, *An Introduction to Phonetics and Phonology,* Oxford : Basil Blackwood Ltd, 1990.

Ewen, J. Colin and Ellen M. Kaisse (eds.). 1995, *Phonology* 12, No.3, Cambridge: O.U.P.

Giegerich, H.J., 1992, *English Phonology,* Cambridge : O.U.P.

Jakobson, Roman, Gunnar Fant and Morris Halle, 1952, *Preliminaries to Speech Analysis,* Mass : MIT Press.

____________ and Morris Halle, 1956, *Fundamentals of Language, The Hague : Mouton.*

Kiparsky, P., "Some Consequences of lexical phonology", *In Phonology Yearbook 2* : 85-138, 1985.

4

Communicative English: A Pragmatic Perspective

Chhayakanta Sarangi

For a long time the Indian teachers have been following the content-based approach to the teaching of English. They have aimed at teaching English to make the students familiar with the texts, which have moral, religious, cultural and historical value. But today text can mean any piece of language, both written and spoken, which is used for meaningful communication in some real situation. This paper tries to define communicative English and shows its relevance to everyday practical purposes.

No doubt, literary English has aesthetic value, but English rich in literary texts is relevant only to those few students who want to study English literature as a specialised discipline. In these days of globalisation we need to communicate with other countries of the world in the fields of science, technology, commerce, etc. As English has now become a world language, teaching communicative English should be given more importance than literary English.

Communication is a word of Latin origin. It means sharing information or intelligence. Communication is not possible without cooperation between the speaker and the listener, or the sender and the receiver of a message. If the listener does not understand the language of the speaker, no communication will take place. The failure of communication occurs, because the speaker may have used inappropriate language to convey his ideas or the listener may not have been able to understand the message properly. Therefore, a great deal of importance is attached to the skill in the art of communication in all spheres of life.

Communicative English must have grammaticality, acceptability and appropriateness. Grammar, as Palmer says, is not to be found in books, written down or learnt by heart. It is wrong to see grammar as a set of normative rules, which tell us how we should speak or write. Normative grammar teaches us to say, " It is I" instead of "It is me". It teaches us the difference between "owing to" and "due to" or "each other" and "one another". But Palmer says that what is correct or what is incorrect is ultimately a matter of what is accepted by society. This acceptability is very important, because language is a matter of conventions within society. If everyone says, " It is me", it is correct English. The one time rule that "each other" refers only to two, and that for more than two "one another" must be used is no longer strictly observed. "Three men distrusted each other" is now accepted as correct. In the same way the rule that "everyone" or "everybody" is used with singular pronoun " his" or "her" is no more strictly observed. The plural pronoun "their" has been more common in British English today. This acceptability is an important factor in communicative English.

To use a language properly we have to know the grammatical structure of the language, but we should also know what forms of language are appropriate in a particular situation. There are varieties of English such as American English, British English, Indian English, formal English, informal English, etc. These labels remind us that English is not a single language. There are many Englishes each of which belongs to a particular geographical area or a particular kind of situation. However, all these varieties have some general features, which belong to the common core of language. The words children, offspring and kids can be taken as examples to trace the common core term. "Offspring" is formal and used of both animals and human beings. "Kids" is informal and familiar. When we are in doubt, it is safest to use the common core term " children". In the same way we should use a common core construction so far as grammatical viewpoint is concerned. Let us take the following examples:

1. Feeling exhausted, John went to bed early.
2. John went to bed early, because he felt exhausted.
3. John felt exhausted, so he went to bed early.

The first sentence is formal and the third is informal whereas the second one can be used in both speech and writing. It is a common core construction fit for communicative English.

A very common cause of bad speaking or writing is the use of the wrong variety for a particular occasion, using slang on a formal occasion or failing to use slang on an informal occasion. There are so many different purposes, and each purpose calls for a different variety of the language. The type of language, which we use publicly for some serious purpose such as in official reports, letters, etc., which are generally in written forms is called formal English. Informal English is the language of private conversation and of personal letters, etc. The following two sentences can be taken as examples to distinguish between the two labels:

1. When his dad died, John had to search for another job.
2. On the decease of his father, John was obliged to seek alternative employment

The first sentence can be used in a casual conversation between two friends, but the second one is very formal. There are differences of vocabulary between formal and informal language, and communicative English takes note of these differences.

Communicative English keeps in view the person who to speak to. Language tends to be more polite when we talk to a person whom we don't know well or a person senior to ourselves in terms of age or social position. On the other hand, when we talk to a person with whom we are familiar or who is junior to us in terms of age or social position, language becomes familiar or informal. In some languages there are special familiar pronouns, but English has no such pronouns. Politeness is expressed in English through the right choice of modals. For examples:

Open the door, will you?

Would you please open the door?

Would you mind opening the door?

The first request is familiar or informal, the second one is polite, and the third one is more polite.

Communication is an art, and the speaker is sometimes required to be tactful if he wants to avoid causing offence or distress to someone. For instance, if we want to avoid mentioning the unpleasant fact of someone's death, we can say, "Smith's father passed away." Let us take another example form another situation. Miss Smith is a typist, and it is her duty to obey me and type my letter. If I say to her, "Type this letter", it may sound harsh to her, and she may not comply with my request. But if I say, "Would you like to type this letter for me?" I disguise my order, and thereby I may win her cooperation more readily.

Language is a form of human social behaviour. Therefore, it is natural that there should be varieties of languages. Communities split up into groups and each group displays differences of behaviour. Language reflects these differences. The primary function of language is to convey ideas from one person to another, but these ideas may be information, command or request. Language should be used to make it clear whether we are well-disposed or ill-disposed towards the person we are speaking to.

Different speakers of English vary greatly in the extent of their vocabulary and in their skill in using it. Like Indian languages English has also dialects. A group of speakers with some non-linguistic characteristics in common may speak a dialect. The most commonly shared characteristic is a regional one. People who live in the same place tend to talk alike. But instead of being regional, the link may be social or occupational, too. Sometimes a variety of language depends not on the people who use it, but on the occasion when it is used. The same man may use widely different varieties of language when he speaks on the telephone, addresses a public meeting and talks to his wife. Such varieties have been called situational dialects.

In communicative English there should not be any attempt to translate those regional words, which do not have equivalents in English from the cultural point of view. An Indian trying to speak to someone about *dharma, yajna, chappati*, etc., should not use such words as religion, sacrifice and bread respectively. The word "sacrifice" does not mean what we actually mean by *yajna*. Therefore, communicative English emphasises the direct use of culture-specific words as they are in the regional languages, otherwise no real communication can take place. Moreover, even complex idiomatic expressions may also stand in the way of communication. Expressions like "raining cats and dogs", "leaving no stone unturned" can be taken as examples in this respect.

English in India is no more the language of the alien rulers. It has been accepted as an Indian language by the Sahitya Academy since 1960. In a multilingual country like India English serves as lingua franca. People of different regional languages can exchange their thoughts and ideas through English and benefit by it. In this respect, communicative English plays a very important role in India. Now a lot of books are being translated from various regional languages into English. The exchange or thoughts through English will definitely help broaden the horizon of literature as a whole. But unless English that is used in translation is communicative, the objective of translation will be defeated. On the whole, the art of writing or speaking should be like a window of plain glass through which the writer's or speaker's meaning becomes clearly visible.

References

Brook, G.L, *Varieties of English,* London: The Macmillan Press Ltd, 1973.

Leech, Geoffrey and Jan Svartvik *A Communicative Grammar of English,* U.K.: ELBS, 1975.

Palmer, Frank, *Grammar,* London: Penguin Books, 1971.

Rao, S.S Prabhakar, *English for Professional Students,* Hyderabad: The Hi Tech Publishers, 2000.

Sharma, R.C. & Krishna Mohan, *Business Correspondence and Report Writing,* New Delhi: Tata MCGraw Hill Publishing Company Ltd, 1994.

Wood, F.T. *Current English Usage* (revised by R.H. Flavell & LM Flavell), London: Macmillan Publishers Limited, 1981.

5

Communication —Breaking the Cultural Boundaries

C.D.Panda

Language use in multilingual and multicultural India is naturally diverse. Although each state in India is carved out based on the dominant language of the region, any school or work environment is also multilingual and multicultural. In such a complex environment, language of knowledge and the culture language may come into conflict with each other and hinder inter-community and intra-community communication. Likewise, because each organisation is hierarchically structured, messages and instructions always do not get passed on in consonance with the intent of meaning. Industry in India has changed over time. Quality, price, service and guarantees, skilled manpower have added new dimensions to the concept of 'competition'. Given the fact that the language of knowledge in the industries is English and interaction is carried on as a mix of English with the local language, distortion of meaning across the hierarchy is apparent. A thorough knowledge of English language, its diverse use, pronunciation, and presentation skills is a must for any successful personality, specially the technocrats. As its a known fact that 89 per cent of technical communication in the world standards is done in English, engineering graduates must have the command over the language.

Multilingualism and language diversities are the need of the day as we all agree. Teachers have to keep in mind that gone are the days of traditional teaching methods where teaching was unipolar. Now, in the bipolar methods of teaching, the teacher has to be aware that for him, communication skill is a must, and that his interpersonal skills affect the students to a great extent. For effective teaching, he must follow certain principles like:

— A learner- and learning-centred approach—a move from teaching to learning.
— A communicative and task-based approach with authentic communication tasks and learning tasks.
— Emphasis on developing language skills and strategies.
— Emphasis on learning to learn, encouraging creativity.
— ESP in higher classes—better preparation for work or study tasks.
— More intensive use of the modern language in the classroom developing language awareness.
— Variety in working methods.
— Use of information technology, multimedia, e-mail, etc.
— Encouraging learner autonomy, self-assessment, cross-cultural awareness.
— Project work (not only traditional tests).

The single most important observation is that the objective of communication is not the transmission but the reception. The whole preparation, presentation and content of a speech must therefore be geared not to the speaker but to the audience. The presentation of a perfect project plan is a failure if the audience does not understand or are not persuaded of its merits. A customer's tour is a waste of time if he leaves without realising the full worth of your product. The objective of communication is to make your message understood and remembered. The theme is that communication education is vital to the development of the whole person. Educators and researchers within and without the discipline attested to the role of communication in self-development. As a discipline which enhances relationships with one's self, others, and society, communication is viewed as central to general education requirements. Communication should be included in early childhood education and should continue through adult education. Students recognise the importance of communication education, but may underestimate the importance of some skills. Communication education improves specific skills and abilities including critical thinking, media literacy and criticism, leadership skills, and family relational development. Educators understand the importance of communication and that acquiring communication knowledge allows one to gain personal power. Communication is vital to the continuation of our society and to erasing cultural boundaries. Education in communication allows the development of skills and sensitivities that shape our social and political lives. Through communication instruction, we develop the ability to speak, which qualifies us to participate in public life. Effective family communication is a deterrent to delinquency and non-verbal communication influences legal decisions.

Communication is a complex interactive process, involving shared assumptions and unspoken agreements between individuals. Understandably, there are frequent errors and misunderstandings in communication. Several types of barriers prevent us from transmitting our ideas meaningfully. Effective communication is very much needed at all the stages for the students of technical institutions for their success. Communication is the life blood of any business. So, when these students join business concerns or corporations as employees, or when they themselves become the entrepreneurs, they need effective communication. Modern business activities are complex. With rapid globalisation, these have become more complex, indeed. For executing these activities good technocrats are needed as the development of a nation largely depends on them. Technological development leads to other developments. Communication skill is an important job requirement nowadays. Some areas like personnel, public relations, marketing, sales, labour relations, call for exceptional communication skills. In the same way, technocrats and researchers also need it equally well. They need a highly developed ability to communicate as they have to present reports, seminars, etc. Even though they belong to technical fields, for presentation and persuasion they do require the abilities of effective communication. Competence in oral communication – in speaking and listening – is a pre-requisite to students' academic, personal, and professional success in life. Indeed, teachers deliver most instructions for classroom procedures orally to students. Students with ineffective listening skills fail to absorb much of the material to which they are exposed. Their problems are intensified when they respond incorrectly or inappropriately because of poor speaking skills. Students who cannot clearly articulate what they know may be wrongly judged as uneducated or poorly informed. Additionally, some speech styles of students can trigger stereotyped expectations of poor ability: expectations that may become self-fulfilling.

Of equal concern, students who are unable to effectively ask for help from a teacher will not receive it, and typically reticent students progress more slowly despite what may be a normal level of aptitude. As individuals mature and become working adults, communication competence continues to be essential.

Communication skills are required in most occupations. Employers identify communication as one of the basic competencies every graduate should have, asserting that the ability to communicate is valuable for obtaining employment and maintaining successful job performance. The communication skills essential in the workplace include basic oral and writing skills, and the ability to communicate in work groups and teams, with persons of diverse background, and when engaged in problem solving and conflict management.

Given the importance of the ability to communicate competently, the communication discipline should be viewed as central on college campuses. Humans are born with the ability to vocalise, but not with the knowledge, attitudes, and skills that define communication competence. The ability to communicate effectively and appropriately is learned and therefore must be taught. Communication skills are commonly recognised as vital to success in business. Students still often underestimate how essential some of these skills may be to their careers. In particular, this study reveals that business students underestimate how much of their time may be spent in meetings, the importance of international communication skills, how often they may have to interact with other employees, the importance of oral presentations, and the ability to use multimedia technology. A more realistic awareness of the importance of these skills might motivate students to prepare more carefully for their communication lives in the workplace.

Communication education is fundamental to career success and the entire business enterprise. People entering the workforce are assisted by communication skills, and employers endorse communication skills as basic to most jobs. Communicative skill is essential in multiple professional careers including accounting, auditing, banking, engineering, industrial hygiene, information science, public relations, and sales. Upward mobility is more probable as communication skills increase. Business and customer interactions are more satisfying and productive with the development of communication skills. Communication skills are essential to those in human resources development. Both business executives and entrepreneurs benefit from communication education. Good communication skills are becoming a requirement for almost any job, and that corporate leaders and human resources managers are realising the importance of strong interpersonal communication skills to the performance of all employees, not just those in supervisory and managerial positions.

Studies have found that consultants' facilitative characteristics, along with an appropriate use of verbal and non-verbal skills, to be important in the consultation process, especially when counsellors must deal with problematic people. Developing a desirable battery of such characteristics and skills would help both counsellors and their clients. To empower employees while maintaining strong leadership, managers must understand the characteristics of leadership and empowerment. A new generation of corporate leaders relies more on the power of influence to motivate rather than on command and control. Leaders must develop and communicate a vision in a way that includes employees. Communication education is most appropriate and effective when it is taught by faculty trained in the discipline and in departments that are devoted to the study of communication.

The communication discipline is an essential component of the educational enterprise – from preschool to adult education. The field is particularly important in the arena of higher education. Communication is a research discipline that has emerged in importance. Communication curricular revision may be most effective when undertaken in conjunction with other departments. Speaking skills are as essential as writing to business communication education. While professional colleges provide a special setting for communication study, these colleges cannot deliver essential communication education by themselves. Communication education is central to all disciplines, and communication administrators know how communication programmes can survive in difficult circumstances. The results of the studies reported herein clearly indicate that communication education develops the whole person, improves the work of education, advances the interests of society, bridges cultural differences, and advances careers and the work of business. That being the case, it is essential that communication curricula should be led and taught by specialists trained in the discipline and in departments that are dedicated to the study of communication. Communication will be one of the most essential skills that students will require when they enter a career path. Finally, communication education serves to enhance our understanding of individuals from multiple cultures.

6

Global Medium and Local Identities: English as a Vehicle of Cultural Enlightenment

Padmini Sahu

Like human beings, language may also be considered a living organism, which is subjected to both decay and development. Total vocabulary of an individual is not constant at any age and time in his lifespan. It is constantly subjected to change. The new experiences may bring subtle changes in the individual's vocabulary by adding some items to his vocabulary. The words that are in his total vocabulary may get deleted because of lack of opportunities for him to use those items, or because of the circumstances, which demand and maintain the use of such items, do not exist any more, or some of the words of the total stock may acquire new meanings.

Similarly, contact with new cultures, new knowledge, and other languages do cause an advent of new concepts into a language, and these concepts are made available to the users of that language through new words or new conventions in the use of existing words. When this contact generally necessitates the mutual flow of ideas and concepts, naturally there will be need for vocabulary that captures these concepts adequately in both the languages.

Just a few centuries ago, English was spoken by just five to seven million people in one relatively small island, and the language consisted of dialects spoken by monolinguals.

Today, there are more non-native than native users of English, and English has become the linguistic key used for opening borders: it is a global medium with local identities and messages. English has become a world language, spoken by at least 750 million people. It is more widely spoken and written than any other language, even Latin, has ever been. It can, indeed, be said to be the first truly global language. English is nowadays the dominant or official language in over 60 countries. The increase in the use of English in Asia is "overwhelming": at present, the estimated population using English in Asia adds up to 350 million. India is the third largest English-using population in the world, after the USA and the UK. Literatures in English are nowadays recognised as part of the national literatures, and English is also recognised in the overall language policy of the nation.

English language has penetrated deeply in the society, which has, in its turn, resulted in several varieties of English in India. The development of those new varieties is connected with historical and social factors. The new varieties of English have all their own contexts of function and usage, and they have also, in their turn, affected the native varieties of English. The use of English clearly increases in the more formal domains. Also, the more formal the situation is, the bigger the number of languages possible for each occasion. In the domains of education, government and employment it is, without doubt, the most preferred medium. It is, however, making its way to more informal domains, as well: about 40 per cent of the informants claim to speak English with friends, and people get introduced to each other most often in English. Over half of all personal letters, too, are written in English. In the neighborhood domain English is the most preferred option when people's languages differ. In the domains of education, government, and employment English shows itself, without doubt, as the most preferred medium.

The questions about language and power go beyond linguistics into history, sociology, attitude studies, politics and economic considerations. The power of language is intimately connected with societal power. It can be manifested by using persuasion, regulation, inducement or force to add a code to a speech community or by the suppression of a particular language variety and the elevation of another. There are two hypotheses concerning language power: the intrinsic-power hypothesis and the acquired-power hypothesis. The first one claims that English would intrinsically possess certain linguistic characteristics, which would make it a preferred language for international purposes. The second hypothesis emphasises the ways in which a language acquires power, and thus it is also easier to understand. This is a fact that English has spread as a result of exploitation and colonisation.

It is notable that, especially in many ex-colonies of Britain, English is still the language of an exclusive social elite. They can be used to expand the speech community, as a vehicle of cultural or religious enlightenment to deculturise people from their own tradition, to gain economic advantage, to control domains of knowledge and information, and for deception.

The first universities were established in India in 1857 (in Bombay, Calcutta and Madras). English became accepted as the language of the elite, of the administration, and of the pan-Indian press. English newspapers had an influential reading public. India, after becoming independent in 1947, was left with a colonial language, in this case English, as the language of government. It was thought that the end of the British Raj would mean the slow but sure demise of the English language in South Asia. This, of course, has not happened. Nationalist imperative wanted that English continue to be used. Nationalist motivations were of the opinion that an indigenous Indian language should be adopted as the official language. Hindi seemed most qualified for that, since it had more native speakers than any other Indian language and was already widely used in inter-ethnic communication. In addition, it was thought that linguistic unity was a prerequisite for political and national unity. Thus, Hindi was designated by the constitution as the language of communication between and within the states. It was to replace English within 15 years. There were, however, several problems with selecting Hindi, and since the protests were often violent (e.g., the riots in Tamil Nadu in May 1963, protesting against the imposition of Hindi), the government wanted to adapt a policy, which would help to maintain the status quo. Firstly, Hindi is not evenly distributed throughout the country, e.g., in Tamil Nadu, in the south, only 0.0002 per cent of the people claimed knowledge of Hindi or Urdu, whereas in the northern states this figure can rise up to 96.7 per cent. Secondly, it was thought that the speakers of other languages would be offended by its selection; other Indian languages, for example Tamil and Bengali, had as much right to be national languages as Hindi. The other Indian communities felt they would be professionally, politically and socially disadvantaged were Hindi, given the central role. Thirdly, Hindi was thought to need vocabulary development before it could be used efficiently as a language of government. In spite of these problems, Hindi was chosen as the national language in the constitution, and English was to be replaced by Hindi in 15 years' time. However, due to the continuous opposition in the south, this replacement was not politically possible. In 1967 a law was passed which allowed the use of both Hindi and English for all official purposes— and that situation still exists.

English is virtually the first language for many educated Indians, and for many, who speak more than one language, English is the second one. Indian speakers of English are primarily bi- or multilingual Indians who use English as a second language in contexts in which English is used among the Indians as a "link" or an "official" language. Only a minimal fraction of the English-using Indian population has any interaction with native speakers of English.

In India, English gradually acquired socially and administratively the most dominant roles: the power and prestige of language was defined by the domains of language use. Ultimately, the legal system, the national media and important professions were conducted in English. Skilled professional Indias became the symbol of Westernisation and modernisation. Raja Rammohan Roy was committed to the idea that the "European gentlemen of talent and education" should be appointed to instruct the natives of India. English came to be used by Indians, as well. By the 1920s English had become the language of political discourse, intranational administration, and law, a language associated with liberal thinking. Even after the colonial period ended, English maintained its power over local languages. English was eventually used against Englishmen, their roles and intentions, as it became the language of resurgence of nationalism and political awakening: the medium, ironically, was the alien language. Mohandas K. Gandhi (1869-1948), for instance, although struggled to create consensus for an acceptable native variety as the national language, expressed his message to the elite in English.

In India, as in other linguistically and culturally pluralistic societies, the position of English is determined by various political, cultural and social considerations. Here, we have three questions to be considered. The first question concerns the position of English in early and in higher education. The second question is concerned with the roles of the regional language, Hindi and English. The third question deals with the model of English presented to Indian learners, and how that presentation can be made uniformly and effectively. The Government of India has primarily been concerned with the first two questions, which are directly related to language planning at both the national and state levels. In the 1960s a bitter conflict considering the status of various languages in India arose from concerns of the southern states (in which Hindi is not widely spoken) that the use of Hindi in the government services would disadvantage them for employment in those areas. They thought, also, that it was unfair for them having to learn both Hindi and English, whereas native speakers of Hindi would only have to learn English.

Every ten years the literate population of India goes up by about 10 per cent. During its independence, there were only 12 per cent literate Indians, according to the 1991 census there are 52 per cent literate Indians, meaning that over half a billion people are literate. Education is monitored in India by state governments and this finds its expression in different figures for different states. Kerala in south India, with a population of 30 million, has the highest literacy rate in India of about 90 per cent. Rajasthan in north India, with a population of 45 million, has the lowest literacy rate of about 40 per cent. Literacy rate among the urban population is higher than among the villagers. It is also higher among the men than among the women. In some states the gap between literate men and literate women is very salient. For example, in Rajasthan and Bihar, the gap is about 30 per cent, while in Kerala and Mizoram it is about 7 per cent.

Literacy rate among the Scheduled Castes and Scheduled Tribes is lower than in the general population. Among the Scheduled Tribes it is the lowest because many tribes still prefer to stay away from the mainstream population. But since independence the literacy rate among the women and the lower castes has grown up at a much higher rate than among the general population. The state governments allow free education at primary level. But, not all Indians get the opportunity to go to school.

Schools are funded from different sources like government, local bodies and private funds. The smaller the funds the less the students receive. School institutions range from schools without any building to schools with all the hi-tech facilities and even sites on the internet. According to researches made in the 1980s about one-third of Indians study or studied in schools, which have English as medium of instruction. This number went up in the 1990s. For these people, English is in many senses their first language and it is easier for them to read, write and even communicate in English than in their own Indian languages. This makes India the second largest English-speaking country in the world after USA.

At the time of independence in 1947 there were 19 universities in India. In 1997 there were 219 universities or institutions at university levels. The larger universities have many colleges affiliated to them. The language of instruction at the better-rated colleges is English. Among the universities, some universities are considered as high standard good level universities. In 1995 there were over five million students in Indian universities. In general, less then 3 per cent of India's population has academic education, which is very low compared to world standard. But numerically India has almost 24 million university graduates.

English as a prestige language and the tongue of first choice continues to serve as the medium of instruction in elite schools at every level without apology. All large cities and many smaller cities have private, English-language middle schools and high schools. Even government schools run for the benefit of senior civil service officers are conducted in English because only that language is an acceptable medium of communication throughout the nation. Working-class parents, themselves rural-urban migrants and perhaps bilingual in their village dialect and the regional standard language, perceive English as the tool their children need in order to advance. Schools in which English is the medium of instruction are a "growth industry". Facility in English enhances a young woman's chances in the marriage market—no small advantage in the often-protracted marriage negotiations between families. The English speaker also encounters more courteous responses in some situations than does a speaker of an indigenous language.

Works Cited

Bailey, Richard W., Images of English, *A Cultural History of the Language,* Cambridge: OUP, 1991.

Ellis, R., *Understanding Second Language Acquisition*, Oxford: OUP, 1991.

Gardner, R.C., Social Psychology and Second Language Learning, *The Role of Attitudes and Motivation,* London: Edward Arnold Ltd, 1985.

7

Living with Intelligence

G.C.Patro

The life is full of energy and man is blessed with the eternal bliss. One of the most difficult fields of knowledge is to understand our own nature, our weakness and strength. Though man is intelligent enough to handle anything with efficiency yet the polluted thinking of the society has made him unintelligent. Intelligence is never incapable of handling any problem, it is limitless, but unawareness of intelligence is the reason behind all failures.

If we do our work as duty then the element of love is probably lost and the sense of commitment is overshadowed by greed, selfishness and ego. We live in a world where mutual trust is diminishing and the need to believe the self has become obsolete, believing the rest of the world goes still farther from humanity. The degeneration in value system has reduced man to sub-humans with all its sufferings of psychological trauma associated with a fear of failure.

Essence of Intelligence

Life is intelligent undoubtedly. Taking the examples from the living world, everything is blessed with intelligence. The awareness of intelligence may not be with the lower lives as in human beings. The unawareness of intelligence or the awareness of unintelligence is visible in man, may it be man, animal or plants. Probably nobody has ever heard addressing a plant as idiot; or ever seen a cat, dog, or so behaving idiotically excepting human beings.

Intelligence is not an achievement, but understanding intelligence is surely an achievement. The bliss of love, which makes a man committed for the cause of work he undertakes, is probably due to un-recognised Intelligence. Our uninterrupted pseudo learning has interrupted our rational thinking process, thereby damaging pure intelligence. Only human intelligence is said to have damaged or corrupted none else. But there is always a process of undoing the damage, which can be achieved by deep thinking, concentrating, understanding things as they are, mastering the existence of the self and realising the noble. Probably the oriental philosophy has given a therapy to undo the damage of intelligence called meditation.

NATURE OF INTELLIGENCE

It is naturally rebellious and very assertive. It is most individualistic and cannot be restricted to mechanical limitations. It is timeless, limitless and silence. It can only be realised and achieved. Man has always more intelligence than problems. It is a gift of nature.

Intelligence is not greed. It is a perfect satisfaction. Greed is a bi-product of fear and sense of insecurity. No intelligent man can ever be greedy. Intelligent man looks at life and its limitlessness. He may not be a perfectionist but definitely a realistic.

A child is born intelligent, but we make him unintelligent by creating fear in him. He is born unafraid of anything. But our teachings to cope up with life have taught him fear. Education never makes anybody intelligent but intelligence makes one educated, understanding, creative, assertive, productive and possessive.

FEAR FACTOR

Fear is like rust to intelligence, which destroys the courage, the desire to win and the will to rise in a man. This knowledge may make somebody feel that he is wiser than earlier, but practising this is more important than agreeing. Anyone who ignores this cannot believe in objective thinking.

Conclusion

The trust in the 'self' is probably the most important thing, as one is the closest to oneself rather than anybody else. If anybody fails to trust his self, he can never trust anybody or be trustworthy. Intelligence is trust in one's own being. It is an adventure, the thrill and joy of living in the present without craving for the future or bothering about the past. To make the utmost use of the present or living in the present is a challenge and man can do it if he lives with intelligence.

8

Role of Educational Technology in the Education of Low English Proficient Students

P.K. Subudhi and *P.C. Mishra*

Recent years have shown an explosion of interest in using computers for English language teaching and learning. A decade ago, the use of computers in the English language classroom was of concern only to a small number of specialists. However, with the availability of multimedia computing and the internet, the role of computers in English language instruction to Low English Proficient (LEP) students has now become an important issue for large numbers of English language teachers throughout the world.

Particularly multimedia applications dedicated to learning have been available since the early 1990's. The use of the computer with English language learners are by no means new and has been creatively employed in the English language learning context in a variety of ways, for example, multimedia software presents the latest advances by providing an environment in which the traditional English language teaching media of text, pictures, graphics, tasks, sound and video can be incorporated. This paper begins with an introduction and discusses some of the reasons why it is essential understand the use of technology for potential impact on English language teaching and learning.

INTRODUCTION

Between 2000 and 2004, the percentage of colleges with computers intended for instruction grew almost 20 percent to 75 percent. Teachers in public and private colleges use computers and related technologies. With so many computers in the colleges, one might expect computers to be deeply integrated into the educational process, including classes for Low English Proficient (LEP) students. Yet, although all teachers use computers, only 10 per cent of the regular teachers who teach LEP students use computers. The role computers and other educational technologies play in educating LEP students will be examined in this paper.

Computers can no longer be relegated to the role of drill master for those students not achieving proficiency in a subject or as a reward for those who do. Arguments that either the hardware or the software have been inadequate are no longer valid. There have been significant advances in such areas as the processing speed, sound, graphics, and video capabilities of computers. These technological advances in hardware and software have exciting potential applications in educating LEP students. Teachers, administrators, and others involved in the education of LEP students are now able to take advantage of these technological advances.

Effectiveness of Computers for Teaching LEP Students

The two basic technologies represented in the sample were video and computer use. The study found that technology can have a significant positive effect on LEP students. Video technology enhanced instruction because:

— bidirectional television made scarce teaching resources available to students that were geographically dispersed;

— and the use of videotapes brought the outside world into the classroom while giving the teacher a versatile tool that [could] play real life situations, stopping, starting, and replaying as needed to clarify or reinforce specific issues.

According to the review study, while video technology can augment traditional teaching, computer technology can bring a "revolution" in teaching. This is because computers have the potential for permitting students to learn at their own speed in a highly motivating and non-threatening environment. The major impediments to the effective use of computers in the colleges is the lack of instructionally and technologically sound software and the lack of training in the planning for and use of computers.

Some researchers provided a comprehensive review of the literature on technology in the colleges and analysed trends in the distribution of computers, computer access, sources of variation in access, equity issues, racial and ethnic differences, instructional applications of computers, teacher training and experience, and the effects of computers in education.

Although the research tends to support the continued use of instructional technologies in the colleges, the study results are mostly subjective. Furthermore, there have been no comprehensive national studies which focus exclusively on the effectiveness of educational technologies for LEP students.

To ascertain direct measures of effectiveness, researchers must review more rigorous experimental studies which compare the achievement of students using computers to those not using computers. It is found that many of the earlier studies examined the use of mainframe or minicomputers, not microcomputers (which are found in most colleges today). Moreover, software design and use have changed significantly over the last few years. More research is needed to determine under what conditions and circumstances computers can be effective

Types of hardware configurations in Use in the Education of LEP students

Computer hardware is the machinery or equipment that allows the software to operate and often consists of a central processing unit (cpu) or the "brain" of the computer, a monitor (the screen), a keyboard, and a printer.

There is a great diversity of hardware configurations currently being used in colleges. Basically, however, they can be divided into two categories: stand-alone computers or computers that are linked together as a network. The majority of colleges use a stand-alone approach, where each workstation has an independent computer system with a single keyboard, monitor, and one or two disc drives.

The placement of stand-alone computers in colleges differs greatly. In some colleges, each classroom may have one or two computers, whereas in other colleges, the computers are centrally located in one computer laboratory. Many colleges that do not have the luxury of having enough computers to place a computer in each classroom keep their computers in a lab.

Developing a computer lab requires planning to handle the logistics of scheduling computer use by students, to assure that equipment and materials are available and to incorporate the computer use into lesson plans (Fluton 1988). Although teachers may intend to meet regularly with the computer lab staff to coordinate lessons and content materials, this initial enthusiasm can dwindle quickly. Many teachers use the time when their students are at the computer lab for an additional planning period or free period; instead, teachers could be using this computer time as an opportunity to learn with the students. Not all teachers have the time or resources to take computer classes in addition to teaching full time. Learning is a cooperative activity, and learning about or with a computer is one activity that both teachers and students can enjoy together.

Computer networks involve connecting several workstations together with cables, so that individual workstations are dependent upon a master workstation. This method of instruction is initially more expensive than the stand-alone approach, but as the number of workstations increases, networking becomes a more economical approach than an equal number of stand-alone workstations. However, the cost effectiveness of networked stations may be lost if the expense of installing cables to connect the workstations is high.

Use of Emerging Technologies in the Education of LEP Students

There are several emerging technologies which have potential applications for the education of LEP students. The use of videocassette recorders (VCRs), optical-disc technology, such as Compact Disc Read Only Memory (CD-ROM), and interactive videodisc systems will be discussed below.

Videocassette Recorders

The use of videocassette recorders is becoming increasingly common in the education of LEP students. Since many teachers and administrators are familiar with the technical aspects of VCRs, their use has been readily accepted. In some college systems, students are allowed to borrow English tapes to view at home.

CD-ROM

Compact Disc Read-Only Memory (CD-ROM) systems use technology which was developed for the audio compact disc industry. These systems store 550 million bytes (a byte is a group of eight "bits" or two digit units, and microcomputer memory capacity is measured in the number of bytes of information it can store) on 4.7-inch discs. In other words, one CD-ROM disc can hold up to 250,000 pages of text (Kuhn, 1987).

CD-ROM systems can be used in education for storing and retrieving large databases, particularly in college libraries. For example, Grolier's Encyclopedia, Encyclopedia Brittanica, Webster's Unabridged Dictionary and Random House Dictionary are currently available on CD-ROM. Educational Resources Information Clearinghouse (ERIC), a database on educational research and practices, is also available on CD-ROM format.

In the future, when more libraries will use CD-ROM technology for storing large bodies of information, intermediate or advanced LEP students may benefit from exposure to this medium. For example, these students may use CD-ROM technology to provide them with information for book reports or essays. However, students may not be able to benefit as much, since much of the information stored on CD-ROM systems requires a high level of English proficiency.

VIDEODISCS

The use of videodiscs, or interactive video, is another emerging technology which has great potential for the education of LEP students. Videodisc systems store video pictures, still pictures, and sound on discs that users can control with a videodisc player or, in some sophisticated systems, with microcomputers (Brandon, 1988). These systems can provide the interactive capabilities of computers and the motion-picture capabilities of videos. For LEP students, interactive video is particularly appropriate because it can create a multisensory, multidimensional language centre that is specially tailored to their needs. With interactive video, students can extrapolate information from contextual and non-verbal cues in addition to reading. Interactive video can be an excellent instructional delivery system for LEP students because it:

— enhances cooperative learning, offers the drama of live-action video, provides immediate feedback, elicits overt behaviours, and makes reading an active and interactive process.

— combines text, graphics, animation, audio, still frame slides and moving video segments in any combination.

— can be used for individualised remediation (Katsareas, 1988).

Two videodisc programmes which have been used with LEP students include PALS and Skillpac. The Principle of Alphabet Literacy System (PALS) is an IBM interactive videodisc programme which teaches literacy to adults. PALS was designed to teach basic literacy to low literate or illiterate native English - speaking adults. The first phase of PALS uses a fictionalised story of the invention of the alphabet in 3100 B.C. Some instructors have commented that the vocabulary of the PALS myth is too idiomatic for the low literate or illiterate non-native English speaker (Katsareas, 1988).

Skillpac: English for Industry is another interactive videodisc system which has been used with LEP students. Skillpac teaches English and cultural skills in a vocational context appropriate for the petroleum, construction, and other industries. Different versions for native Spanish and Portuguese speakers have been used with displaced workers in Massachusetts. Skillpac may be useful with LEP students at the college level in technical education classes, since the materials provide visual images as well as opportunities for listening in context, which is critical for effective language learning (Grognet, 1987).

Computers That Talk: Speech Recognition Devices

In recent years, the speech capabilities of computers have increased dramatically, and many computers that "talk" no longer sound like robots. Digitised voice attachments are available for most computers, but there is a great diversity in the quality of speech; some computers sound more like human voices than others. This is because the speed of processing (including the storage capacity of the system) and the type of processing vary. However, at the present time, there is a time lag between the availability of the digitized voice attachments and software which capitalises upon the new speech voice capabilities of computers. LEP students would be able to hear what they have written on the computer screen in addition to seeing it. The advanced voice capabilities of computers will greatly enhance English instruction as more "talking" software becomes available.

Writing to Read is an example of a programme which uses the capabilities of an IBM Personal Computer with a digitised voice attachment. Writing to Read has received nationwide attention and has been implemented in college systems across the country; administrators and teachers have consistently reported dramatic results. In 1988, IBM released a manual of the Writing to Read programme adapted for LEP Student, developed by Dr. John Henry Martin. One of the reasons for this programme success with LEP students may be that it is a multimedia, multifaceted instructional delivery system consisting of five components: (1) Computer Station, (2) Work Journal Station, (3) Listening Library Station, (4) Writing/Typing Station, and (5) Make Words Station.

Some of the educational principles and practices that make Writing to Read effective for language acquisition are as follows:

- It operates in a positive, highly supportive environment which models language rather than corrects it.
- Students can progress at their own pace and control their own learning.
- Personal experiences and cultures are valued and used as a context for listening, speaking, reading, and writing.
- The programme emphasises concrete, multisensory activities.
- The programme takes a developmental rather than a remedial approach to learning.
- The computer and other learning materials are used for skill development, creativity of expression, interaction, and natural communication.
- Listening is considered basic to learning, and a variety of listening opportunities are provided.
- The programme capitalises on existing language skills and does not demand that students read or write anything they cannot say or understand.

Types of Software Available and how are Their Use in the Education of LEP Students

There is a variety of software available for use with LEP

students. The software, which gives the computer instructions (and is often thought of as the material which is on the floppy disc), has been grouped into the following five major categories: drill and practice, tutorials, simulations, games, and applications. The types of software are described below, along with possible applications for the instruction of LEP students.

Drill and Practice

The most common type of instructional software used in education, (including the education of LEP students) is drill and practise. Moreover, low-achieving students use computers to practice and reinforce basic skills (which are often the focus of drill and practice programmes), while high-achieving students concentrate more on programming and problem-solving skills.

Drill and practice software is often described as the "electronic textbook", where students can work on questions and answers, substitutions, or completion exercises and answer by typing a letter, number, word, phrase, short sentence, or lines of text (Cubillos, 1984). Although drill and practice software is not the most interesting form of interactive instruction, it is still useful. For example, if one student needs additional practice on the past tense in English grammar, and another student has mastered the past tense but needs reinforcement with the future tense, drill and practice software programmes can provide both students with as much reinforcement as necessary at the same time. The computer will continue to review the same material over and over again until each student has mastered the concept that needs reinforcement, whereas the classroom teacher may not have sufficient time or patience. In many instances, English classrooms have students with different proficiency levels; students can work at their own level on the computer to reinforce the principles the teacher has taught (while the teacher can continue to work with those students who have the most difficulties).

Drill and practice software has become increasingly sophisticated over the years. In many cases, teachers can create their own vocabulary lists and individualise the content of the lesson. Also, many programmes provide record-keeping procedures where teachers can review the progress of individual students.

Drill and practice in its most positive application can give students more time on a task: students can practise at their own pace without pressure until they fully master the concept. However, some educators feel that this type of software provides less instruction than a classroom teacher who can provide constant human interaction.

Tutorials

Tutorials are similar to drill and practice programmes, except that they have the additional capability of branching to various areas, depending upon students' individual needs. For example, if a student has answered several questions in a row incorrectly, the programme may branch into an easier group of questions. On the other hand, if a student answers several questions in a row correctly, the programme may branch into more difficult questions. Tutorials, unlike drill and practice, actually tutor, so that they teach concepts and provide explanations. They capitalise on the ability of the computer to individualise instruction to meet the unique needs of each learner.

Simulations

Simulation software simulates actual situations and can be used for classroom activities. Simulations are particularly common in the sciences, where it is sometimes difficult to provide real-life experiences. For example, the software programme called Operation Frog allows students to dissect a frog on the computer. Simulations can be particularly useful in the education of LEP students, since there is often a shortage of science equipment and supplies designed for them. However, many simulations are complicated programmes which require a high level of English proficiency to operate, making them difficult for some LEP students. Simulations could be used more widely if the software had simpler directions for LEP students. Many teachers make their own summary sheets of how to use the software. These summaries can be used in English instruction as well as to provide better operating instructions for the students. More simulation software is needed for the LEP population, but simulations often require more computer memory than do other software programmes, and thus may tax the limits of many colleges' equipment.

Games

Educational games, which provide instruction as well as entertainment, are another type of software. Generally, educational games are designed to take advantage of the graphic capabilities of the computer, which tend to engage students. Educators must take care to find games which are educational; often students want to play computer games which are only entertainment. Educational games can be used effectively with LEP students because there is often less text on the screen than with other software programmes. For example, beginning students who do not have many English language skills can benefit from educational games, where instruction is reinforced through graphics.

Applications

Software applications include databases, spreadsheets, programming, authoring languages and authoring systems, and word processing. Databases, which can be thought of as computerised card catalogues (with each card in the catalogue similar to one computer record), can be used to teach concepts such as categorisation and grouping. An example of this can be found in the National Clearinghouse for Bilingual Education Program Information Guide No.5, using Computer Concepts as Problem-Solving Tools in the Language Classroom (1988), which provides instruction on using these concepts in mathematics classes. With the use of databases, students can learn many skills at the same time such as grouping, the content of the groups, and vocabulary, as well as the computer skills necessary to manipulate the information in a database. Spreadsheets, often thought of as computerised account ledgers, can be used to teach mathematics skills and to practise computations. In addition, spreadsheets can provide older LEP students with practical survival skills such as monthly budgeting and accounting.

In the early years of computing, instead of using the computer to work with content areas, programming was the most common use of the computer. Programming, where students give instructions to the computer that are converted through the programming language into individual machine instructions, controls the operation of the computer. The early emphasis on programming stems from the fact that most computer teachers were programming enthusiasts themselves, and there was little educational software available. Moreover, in the past, computer lab coordinators in many schools were mathematics teachers, since they were required to take one or two programming courses as part of their mathematics certification.

Use of Technology to teach Reading-Writing Skills to LEP Students

The debate over what types of software should be used in schools and how they should be used (such as teaching programming or word processing) brings up the question of whether software should be used as an instructional tool or an intellectual tool. Software which is instructional merely "instructs", while software which is an intellectual tool is used to develop critical thinking skills or problem-solving skills. Ideally, software should be both instructional and intellectual. However software is used, it should be emphasized that, "technology does not supplant the teacher, but instead provides teachers with new methods and teaching tools. Technology cannot make a poor teacher into a good teacher. Technology can increase the effect and effectiveness of a good teacher, and can make a good teacher a better teacher."

For LEP students in particular, using word processing and computers has great potential for developing both reading and writing skills. Since the teacher or lab coordinator must provide the text (content) which will be used in word processing, this type of instruction may be difficult for new teachers to implement initially. However, it can be cost effective since the programme itself can be used for many different content areas (unlike, for example, a drill and practice programme on adjectives).

Besides the instructional potential of word processing, there are several other advantages to this application: it is relatively inexpensive; it is easy to use; it requires no programming knowledge and limited computer experience; and it is not threatening to most students or teachers. Moreover, since word processing is a skill which many students will need to succeed in the workplace, many of them are especially interested in receiving this type of instruction.

In *Microcomputers and English Language Instruction: A Few Years Later,* Jex describes the use of the word processor to achieve two instructional goals at the same time: language instruction and word processing. Some examples of the dual functions of the word processor include:

1. At the most basic level of English instruction, teachers can create cloze, fill-in-the-blanks, or matching exercises. Students can complete the exercises both on-screen and on print-outs. For example, students can review grammar while learning basic word processing tasks.
2. Once students have mastered the most basic word processing commands, then they can expand their practice to include editing larger language elements. Students can create paragraphs from scrambled sentences while practising moving small blocks of text with the word processor.
3. When students become comfortable with manipulating small blocks of text, they can refine their organising skills in preparation for writing. Students can organise sentences or paragraphs into categories such as theme, thesis, and support.

4. Finally, students can shorten, edit, and summarise full-length documents (or essays) using the cut/paste commands. Although beginning students may not have the English language skills necessary to edit long essays or even paragraphs, most educators agree that students are more "engaged" in their learning activities, regardless of the content, when using the computer. In writing, for instance, students seem to write more (judging by word count) when they are writing on the computer. More is not always better, but it is often easier to delete or edit text than it is to create text from scratch. Also, if students are having difficulty in penmanship, the computer allows them to concentrate on the content of the writing as opposed to the act of writing itself. Many times, this improved concentration on content can greatly affect the students' work and general interest in writing.

The use of the computer as an interactive instructional medium can complement the reading-writing process. Using the word processor to teach writing skills obviously involves reading, whether or not reading is identified as the specific area of concentration. Reading and writing (especially original writing) is often a joint process. If the examples of word processing are analysed, it is clear they require both reading and writing skills to perform successfully. In summary, the reading-writing process, when effectively combined with the capabilities of the computer, can greatly enhance English instruction.

Factors affecting Successful Implementation of Technology

In most studies of the implementation of new innovations in education, the teacher is identified as the participant who is most closely associated with the success or failure of the implementation of new technology. The teacher can encourage or discourage, help or hinder, integrate the computer into the regular classroom activities or isolate it (Schcolnik, 1987). However, the implementation of technology is also affected by other factors which will be described below.

Lack of Appropriate Software

The most common complaint among educators implementing computers in the classroom is that there is a lack of appropriate software. Many new, excellent programmes have been developed in the fields of mathematics, sciences, language arts, social studies, and foreign languages, as well as software utility packages, such as word processing and spreadsheets, which can be used in a variety of content areas. For the LEP students, however, the lack of software is still a concern. In the fields of English education, the quantity and quality of software designed especially for LEP students lag far behind software developed for other subjects.

Software not often Integrated into Curriculum

Not only is there a need for appropriate software for LEP students, but such software would be more useful if it were integrated into the curriculum. However, a software that is designed to reinforce discrete tasks is sometimes difficult to integrate. For example, a programmed which reinforces the past tense may not warrant the preparation time necessary for its successful implementation. Since time and materials are expensive, teachers must look for software which can teach a variety of language skills; a teacher would not use a textbook simply because it reinforces the past tense in English without teaching additional language skills. In time, however, it is expected that more software will become integrated into the curriculum. Educators must remember that the use of computers in the colleges is a relatively new technology and it will take time to fully integrate it.

Lack of Compatibility between Hardware and Software or between Hardware Components

Selecting the appropriate mix of hardware and software is vital to the successful implementation of computer technology in an instructional programmed. As in the selection of personal computers for home use, buyers must consider a number of factors such as how the computer will be used, how much memory is required to use programmes or applications, and whether or not the system can be upgraded by adding peripherals. Colleges must plan ahead and purchase equipment which will continue to meet their computer needs. Anticipating the changes in the needs of the students (for example, selecting computers which are easily upgraded and/or expanded to handle additional memory as the computer applications become more complex and require additional memory) is necessary to ensure the successful utilisation of technology.

Lack of Teacher Training

A major cause of the difficulties in the implementation of technology is the lack of sufficient teacher training, both preservice and inservice. If teachers are to successfully integrate computers in their classroom, teachers themselves must learn about computers. In many school districts, when the computer "guru" (the expert teacher or the one enthusiast who seems to know everything about computers) leaves the school system, the rest of the programme suffers. Without proper direction and training, the instructional programme dwindles until another computer expert joins the staff.

To successfully use computers in the education of LEP students, teachers must receive sufficient instruction on the use of computers. Sufficient instruction includes preservice training, inservice training, and continuous support. According to some teacher trainers, teachers have remarked that they were "entertained, not trained". Most teachers are required to have some type of training on computers, but much of this training in the past has been devoted to programming. Teachers need to receive training on how to review and evaluate software for implementation in the classroom as well as how to successfully integrate technology into the curriculum. In addition, teaching with technology requires a different set of skills (the ability to move back and forth between lecturing and coaching) than does traditional instruction. Teacher trainers must provide ample time for teachers to practise these skills.

Recommendations for Future Directions

Additional Teacher Training and Support

Ongoing training and support must be provided in order for the programmes to succeed and maximise the effectiveness of technology as an instructional medium. For example, teachers should be encouraged to take courses related to computers (not just programming) and should be rewarded for their efforts.

Appropriate Software for LEP Population

Colleges could maintain closer ties to the software industry to ensure the appropriateness of product design. The tradition of software being created by programmers who are not practitioners to be used by teachers who do not have expertise in instructional design for technology may not have provided the most pedagogically sound materials.

A possible long-term project for colleges could be to provide grants as seed money to software companies for the development of products. In return, the colleges would field-test the software and then buy it for their district at a discount.

Funding further Research, Including Exemplary Programmes with Computer Components

At the federal and state levels, additional funding could be provided for comprehensive studies on the effectiveness of the various emerging technologies in the education of LEP students, as well as for exemplary programmes which use this technology, such as long-distance learning and interactive videodiscs.

Ensuring Equal Access to Computers

Although some classroom teachers use computers, very less of the regular teachers who teach LEP students use computers. That the percentage of teachers who use computers to teach their LEP students is consistently lesser than the percentage of teachers who use computers to teach other students points to a question of access, both quantitative and qualitative. LEP students need equal access to computers, and more importantly, should have the same qualitative access to computers as other students. All students deserve the same opportunities to use computers with the same computer applications.

Conclusion

This paper highlights some of the current research on the uses of computers in the colleges, the types of software being used in the education of LEP students, some current uses of technology (such as interactive video, word processing, and electronic networks) to teach reading and writing skills, and emerging technologies which may merit future consideration. Further research is needed on a regional or national scale to determine the effectiveness of these various technologies for LEP students. Factors which may affect the implementation of computers for LEP students include the following: lack of appropriate software, lack of integration of software into the curriculum, lack of compatibility between hardware and software or between hardware components, lack of funding to support repairs and maintenance of computer systems, and, perhaps most importantly, lack of teacher training. Although there are many factors which may affect the successful implementation of technology in the colleges, the most important factor in technology is the human factor.

Even if the computer can be beneficial in assisting students to master language skills, it is not the universal panacea, nor is it as versatile as the human teacher. It would be impossible to successfully implement technology in the colleges without the help of caring teachers who can provide the environment which all students need to develop to their full potential.

References

Brandon, Paul R., *Recent developments in instructional hardware and Software,* Educational Technology, 28(10), 7-12, 1988.

Cubillos, Enrique M., What is bilingual education CAI? *Bilingual Journal,* 8 (1-2), 8-12,48, 1983-1984.

Fulton, Kathleen, *Preservice and Inservice: What must be done in both,* Electronic Learning, 8(2), 32-36, 1988.

Grognet, Allene G., Skillpac: English for Industry Washington, DC: Centre for Applied Linguistics, 1987.

Katsareas, Dimitri, Implementation aspects of interactive videodisc technology: A report on the operation of the Skillpac and PALS instructional delivery systems at two adult training sites, the Multicultural Career Intern Programme and the Consortium for Workplace Literacy, Alexandria, VA: Hudson Institute, 1988.

Kuhn, Carolyn, Questions and Answers about CD-ROM, CALICO Journal, 5(1), 73-76, 1987.

Schcolnik, Miriam, RE-WORD CALI: A method practising Reading Skills with the Aid of a Word Processor, CALICO Journal, 5(1), 65-72, 1987.

9

Need of Language Art and Writing Fictions

P.N.Singh

Abstract

This paper presents strategies and activities that stimulate higher level and imaginative thinking in important curriculum extensions in engineering colleges, and exploring the elements to write fictions.

English is an increasingly important global language of communication. Countries that wish to compete in the global economy have a keen awareness of the need for competent English speakers in business, politics and education. Therefore, there is a steady demand for English language in engineering colleges also. It should be for first two semesters in the course as foreign language or second language. Students can be encouraged by expressing their need of the language and arranging extempore debates, group discussions, personality development classes and writing fictions in English to get more command over the language.

Need of Language Art

Instruction must provide students with the techniques and sources that fully engage their analytical minds and imaginative talents. Readers and writers can expand their experience of literature when they respond to it through their own original work—creative writing, designing, composing and dramatising. Higher-level thinking skills of analysis, interpretation and evaluation are inherent to the creative processes described in this digest. When used as a curriculum extension, the strategies are especially for students, and may also be used to teach critical thinking skills to all students of an engineering college.

English language teachers need to have a strong footing in the theory and best practices of language learning and teaching in order to plan and deliver effective English language programmes.

Engineering graduates should be prepared with good knowledge of English as a second/foreign language, both domestically and internationally. In order to ensure that our graduates have the practical skills they need to be successful classroom teachers Two extensive practicum components are integrated with academic study. The practicum components include observation and classroom teaching experience.

Engineering colleges are responding to an increasing demand from international educators and students to offer a formal graduate certificate programme in teaching English as a second language.

The two-semester programme will incorporate both teaching English as a second language and teaching English as a foreign language, providing theory and practical applications for teaching English to students with various backgrounds and at all levels of English proficiency.

Exploring the Elements (by Writing Fictions)

To write, to perform any art, is not merely or even mainly to create—it is to make, it is to work with something, to form it out of materials already at hand. Create cannot help but bring godlike creation to mind, from its ancient relationship. It also, in contemporary conjures the spectre of "creative writing", the genericism that fiction writers and poets have allowed to be foisted on themselves. Mention an interest in creative writing too often and you'll inevitably be asked about your inspiration (or told where you can find some), and with inspiration comes the thought of breathing life into things and, before you know it, your vocation has once again taken leave of this earth.

No, writing is not mainly creating. The idea of creating may be useful for sustaining a certain productive tension, but essentially, it focuses too much attention on the one per cent inspiration in one's soul and too little on the ninety-nine per cent perspiration saturating one's desk. The work's the thing. As I said above, to write is to make, to form something out of materials at hand. Make has a blunt crisp sound I like, a gritty aural texture. It not only alludes to some of the same ideas as create, but also carries connotations of shaping something to one's will and of success (to "make it" is to succeed). The hands are the key. The written word cannot be literally handled, yet words are tools. Many other writers have pointed out that writing is a technology, a technology "for collective memory, for preserving and passing on human experience." One notes that whereas it is easy for us to recognise the traditional and the new ways for distributing and preserving writing—the printing press and the computer—as technologies, writing itself we have so deeply interiorised that it is ironically difficult for to realise that

"Writing is in a way the most drastic of the three technologies. It initiated what print and computers only continue, the reduction of dynamic sound to quiescent space, the separation of the word from the living present, where alone spoken words can exist".

Literature conveys not concepts existing in a void, but concepts worked over to present a richness of felt experience. As one writer suggest, 'texts' in literature 'put' ideas 'in hand', as it were, to frame knowledge within the dramatic fabric of experience, even as the technology of books and book production literally brings ideas 'to hand'.

Divergent Thinking

Exploring the elements can be exciting if students are asked to improvise and think divergently about the stories. All students can benefit from the critical thinking that this strategy demands, and the teacher can adapt it to more difficult content, depending on the ability and grade level of the students. Begin with fundamental questions: If you could change this, what would you change it to? How? Why? Then break down the different elements of a composition and discuss how specific changes would change the whole effect.

Using Fractured Fairy Tales to Explore Fiction

Fractured fairy tales are designed to be humorous by changing a familiar story in an unexpected way, such as altering the plot, a character, or setting. One student might decide to make Little Red Riding Hood a tough, strong girl, completely unafraid of the wolf and able to save her grandmother. Another student may select a fictional superhero and create a humorous flaw that causes problems when he/she has to save the day. When the teacher presents a fractured fairy tale, asking a series of questions helps the students think through the changes and what they mean. Examples include:

— What characters in this story differ from the original and how?

— Which events occur in the new one that doesn't in the original?

— How do the changes in characters and plot in the second one change the meaning and/or the way you feel about the characters?

— How does this change the overall effect?

— What do you think the writer is trying to say in this new version?

When students are asked to change the nature of even a few characters in a fairytale, they will discover that the smallest change can affect the plot. If their changes remove the conflict and suspense from the story, the teacher can take them back to the original story. What moment in the story held the most tension for them? What kept them riveted to the story?

Re-examining their own ideas, students can then identify the areas where the conflict and suspense have gone and can brainstorm ways to create new conflicts. This process can apply to the simplest stories as well as to the most advanced novels and plays. For students, the possibilities are limitless and the problems presented by the process endlessly fascinating. The key is to discuss the relationships across story elements and to examine what is gained or lost with each change.

A Study of Perspective: Biographical and Historical Fiction

Biographies and histories provide rich material for students to re-imagine actual events from new, even unusual, points of view. Students rarely accept anything on face value and enjoy debating points in politics and history based at their own alternate readings of the events. Writing biographical and historical fiction enables them to capitalise on this talent and use it to explore different perspectives both critically and creatively.

Researching Facts

Begin by exposing the students to the life experiences of prominent men and women through books, magazines, and short films, and through pictures, drawings, or images of their work. Ask them what influences in these individuals' young lives affected their development, how they overcame the obstacles or challenges that stood in their way, and what their most significant contributions were. When they write this information down in a paragraph form or as a series of notes and also jot down any questions they have about the person's life, many students find themselves continually going back to do more research as the story develops in more detail. This is one of the great values of biographical (and historical) fiction: it inspires deeper research and a more critical analysis of issues that appear in their story.

Creating a Point of View

Choose a person (or animal or object) in a prominent person's life and describe an event from this perspective. It could be the person's brother, sister, friend, dog, or even his/her favourite pen. As students begin to tell their stories, they discover how individual points of view create a different focus and perspective than the more "objective" biographies that synthesize information from multiple sources.

Historical fiction works in a similar way. For example, the class may study the Civil War period. After the students acquire a detailed understanding of the issues and conflicts between the north and south and events that finally drove the two sides to war, ask them to create a character from this period. The students create a personal history for their imaginary character and write a story or anecdote that could have occurred in the life of this person in this place in this time. Students who use biography and history as a source for creating fiction begin to see history and non-fiction generally in a different light. Within news report or a historical event are many individual lives, each with a slightly different perspective. Perhaps in no other form do critical and creative thinking work so closely. Writers who love history discover a limitless source of material—the stories of many civilisations around the world—that can become the world of their characters, the cause of conflicts, the most suspenseful moments of their own stories. These activities lead to a reflective understanding of how the stories of history are told and how bias can impact the representation of events.

Roots of Writing

Remembering the roots of writing, reconceiving it as a technology, as a way of making texts rather than a way of mimicking a creator, helps one as an artist step beyond the squabbling about what's technological and what's natural and engage the electronic era in a way that truly matters. Here are new tools: how do they affect the way I work with the materials of my craft? The anecdotes and stories, the clutter of mental and physical notes and scraps of information, the readings and re-readings of my own and others' texts, and most of all the words, the words and all their extra-verbal evocations of image and feeling, sensation and thought, remain; and whether I work them, knead them with pencil and paper, ribbon and keyboard, or mouse and window, the craft manifested in the linkages between artist, tool, and work persists in all its intimate symbiosis.

Where do I get my ideas? I pose the question to myself here, to explore how the answer may be altered by the new writing spaces. As I write fiction, I may or may not be aware of the aspects of my artistic world that have sources in my social one. I don't consider myself a particularly autobiographical writer. In most cases anything I use from life is so altered and recontextualised in art that it would be hard for even close friends to detect the source. Yet everything I write has to emerge out of my experience of the world: as I have argued, a writer does not create so much as make, reshape what is already there. The question then becomes: what, exactly, is there?

It is certainly not just stories. Oh, sometimes I get lucky and witness or hear of events that are essentially whole stories, begging to be written down. The events extend across enough time or experiential landscape to take on a narrative shape and reach a closure, even if only an episodic or unsatisfying one. At other times my luck is more mysterious—a plot appears full-blown in my head over the course of a few minutes or hours, source unknown. More often, though, I don't simply find a complete story but catch a whiff of one—an incident, an anecdote, a passing observation of a person or place—that piques my interest enough to make a note of it, mentally or physically. The scraps pile up, and may or may not fit with any other puzzle piece. They may plug right into a story I'm already working on; they may never resonate again for me after that initial moment; or ten years later, as likely as not while I'm sitting in a committee meeting or mowing the lawn, I may suddenly sit up mentally and realise ... oh!

Both of these certainly happen, but they are not all that happens. By themselves they give the impression that ideas for stories are solely a matter of serendipity. But that is far from all. I go looking for them, too—not just stories but the details in which they live and the techniques through which they're told.

Writing is inseparable from reading, not only in the sense of reading other printed materials but in the sense that what I write *is* my reading of my outer and inner worlds. I research topics, more often for non-fiction than for fiction, yet still quite often for either. I also read for pleasure (though I should say that my tastes are affected by my feeling that learning is pleasurable and *not* learning is not). One great writer advised me, "Read at whim! Read at whim!" I take that advice to heart—life is too short (as I am a person with a pace maker in my heart), and I'm too slow a reader, to spend time reading texts like "I am OK, you are OK".

10

Importance of Communicative Approach in Professional and Technical Education

Manas Ranjan Mishra

The sudden realisation by the gurus of management and technocrats that communication is a critical element of life has given rise to a new concept for language studies. The term Communicative English assumes to provide students of professional and technical education its relevance for meaningful purposes in day-to-day life. This paper aims at focusing on the importance of English language study and communication skills for professionals as well as technocrats in the present context.

The pattern of English teaching and learning in India since a long period of time has been traditional in nature. The purposes of teaching English in the past aimed to get the students acquainted with the texts which have something to convey. This traditional method of English studies was meant to learn things in order to communicate it for the teachers, who already know the information. Since here our concern was associated with assessment, we tried to provide all the information in a sophisticated and ornamental language for impression. But in the present set-up where without English we feel helpless, we need to acquire it with little effort.

In the past the technocrats as well as the professionals used to feel that study of English was of no value for them.

They considered it to be an unnecessary burden. But now it has been realised by the established technocrats and business school' guys that success in life is almost impossible without communicative skill. In fact, they realise that in the matter of success in life as well as in business, their so-called 'hard skills' counts only 15percent of their estimated play while the rest attribute to the 'soft skills'.

These professionals encouraged new phenomena towards study of language, which gained immense importance with the growth of the IT sector. The term 'Communicative English' has taken hold because of the revolution in IT sector. The new technology through internet as well as e-mail has given a digital shape to our language. Perhaps the technocrats in this profession momentarily err to feel that they need only the vernaculars for their communication needs. One of the basic features of their communication exhibits emphasis on use of plain language. But when they get exposed to the world community of technocrats they realise the strange burden of lingual simplicity.

The purpose of communication being to convey messages, information or ideas to someone in such a way that he may understand the same does not subscribe to mastery over the language. Moreover, communicative English upholds an ideal of using plain or simple language.

The situation at present is that the better you can communicate your ideas, thoughts, experiences and perceptions the easier it is to succeed in life. A person being unable to express himself appears to be in the most difficult and frustrating situation. With the increasing need of physical movement and information sharing; communication is becoming a basic necessity of life. Expressive manoeuvrability makes a man adaptive and accommodative to new situations arising out of human movements due to increasing need of overseas jobs.

Actually there is no short-cut formula for good communication. To be a good communicator a person has to acquire sound commands over vocabulary. Besides this he must always have his perceptive senses wide open towards the ever-changing world in and around. Effective communication is not a synonym to how many words or expressions one may use. It is rather implies to what words and expressions one selects while communicating.

The language used for communication always plays a vital role. It necessarily doesn't reflect that one needs to make use of difficult words or complicated sentences for achieving impressive needs. The first and foremost objective of communication is to make the receiver understand. The purpose of communication is not to confuse the audience, but to make the receiver accept our information in such a way that he suspends his disbelief and begins to accept our view with some regards. Therefore, its objective being to express in a linear way or in a straightforward manner, it becomes essential to acquire a set of composite skills, one of which is grammatical competence.

Every individual after, several years of study at school or college, inherits a basic knowledge of the grammar of English language. But with that naturally acquired knowledge it appears to be very difficult to use the language fluently while speaking or writing. It may be either because of grammar fatigue or lack of communicative skill. Both these requirements can be fulfilled, but for achieving this one needs to make some conscious, sincere and streamlined efforts. It doesn't mean that one should get on with the books of English grammar for structuring sentences. Since our purpose is to make use of the language, we need to emphasise on the communicative part of English grammar. Actually the basic feature of communicative approach is to enhance the capability of a student in using as well as understanding the spoken as well as the written language. Spoken and written English do not have different grammars, but for such different purposes the same matrix is required to be used differently.

Spoken English gets processed instantly in real time and is transitory, whereas written English consumes time for its production and becomes a permanent record. While speaking, we try our best to convey our ideas in order to be understood at once. Here neither the communicator nor the audience gets time to revise. While writing not only does the writer get time to revise and rewrite, but the reader also gets the chance to re-read and analyse the version. A written word is an orphan because its meaning is subject to interpretation. But a spoken word is legitimate. The speaker is there to protect it's meaning. Perhaps it may be one of the reasons for which people in power never write, they only speak. The spoken word has the metaphysics of presence. Hence it is more authentic than the written word. Therefore, it becomes essential on the part of a person trying to communicate some-thing to choose the channel of communication according to the needs of the situations. Another basic point that should be taken note of is that, before communicating it becomes necessary to know 'what to communicate.' Simply knowing what to communicate will not serve the whole purpose. Besides knowing this one must also be aware of the audience to whom he is going to communicate and how it is to be communicated. Over and above all it must be guided by why to communicate.

A young technocrat or professional may get puzzled because never before was it thought that the skill of communication was so important; but now it is time for them to realise the fact that if they ignore to develop their skills of communication, they cannot have a commanding personality. Since communication has a social parameter, one needs to acquire it for upholding one's integrity. Since the scope of these professionals is not limited to any boundary, it becomes essential for them to acquire the skill of communicating in English, which is the world language. To meet the demands of industry as well as the society communication skill is as valuable as social behaviour.

One of the most important things to remember is that everyone can improve, but for this one has to make a conscious effort. To be a good speaker, one has to be a good listener. Spoken communication needs organisation of ideas and thoughts before delivery. In order to enhance the power of communication one must keep the following things in mind:

— Think before you start speaking.

— Realise the message you want to convey.

— Try to make it easier for the listener to remember your view, by getting on to the point quickly.

— Visualise the outcome of your conversation in a positive manner.

— Make efforts to persuade your audience to accept your point of view.

— Have a plan in your mind about what you want to speak and what you want to achieve.

— Try to have some knowledge about the acceptability perception / ability of your audience.

Fear and nervousness are to some extent obstacles for the beginners trying to communicate in English. Their mind is shadowed with the feelings: "I'll fail", "I can't express what I desire" and "I'll be humiliated for not being a better communicator of my views." But keeping aside all things what ypu have to do is not to think about your, you should rather try to think more and more about the listener or the audience with whom you are going to converse. Secondly, you should think of the message to be conveyed during the course of interaction or conversation and not of the words. If you are clearly aware of your message the words will automatically flow in. Last but not least, while speaking you have to convey that you are speaking from your heart, not from your head. If you are clear in your ideas, thoughts and the message to be conveyed, shape it in such a way that it is easily understood. Further the most important thing to be taken into note is that, you should have complete faith in the message you are going to convey or else you will lose your credibility. If you are not having full faith in what you are going to say, it is better to avoid or remain silent to such topics of discussion. It is only the belief in your ideas or thoughts that makes you speak with passion as well as conviction. Further, it also makes the flow of words and expressions in a natural way matching with the body gestures.

After all the purpose of a particular conversation or communication is to make your idea or message acceptable.

It is better to emphasize on the major points of your topic. If possible try to provide a suitable and familiar examples relating to your topic in order to make the conversation more interesting. As far as practicable clarify your message by delving deep into the issues. Finally frame tactful questions for the listener or audience to get the feedback. Unless you get a feedback, either positive or negative your communication remains incomplete. One thing that is to be kept in the mind is that everyone may not agree with your views and ideas. So, if you get a contrary feedback instead of taking it as a rejection you should accept it as a new response. In order to develop such attitude there are few points to be taken into consideration, which may add something extra into your personality and inter-personal skill:

— Be direct in your approach.

— Be positive about your communicative skills.

— Avoid mental stress and be comfortable.

— Develop a list of positive affirmations showing that what you want already exists.

— Let yourself feel the joy of success.

— Have respect for others.

— Try to avoid words that hurt.

— Be good in manners for establishing a rapport.

— Be flexible in order to have control of the conversation.

— Process your ideas, feelings and information in such a way that you can find agreement.

— Try to eliminate negative feelings.

— Keep smiling and occasionally "poke fun" at yourself.

— Be friendly.

With these things in mind we must try to have two more important things for better communication: sensitivity for acquiring information and clarity for better expression. When we are communicating our expression creates an effect in the mind of our audience. We can put it like this: the language we use creates a kind of stimuli or responses in the audience. If we are unable to make people respond to our views and thoughts then our communication becomes incomplete. Therefore, study of language becomes a matter of paramount importance. It makes us know what to speak and how to speak.

Language and thought are always interlinked. Very few people in their life prove to be naturally gifted with the skill of communicaton. For them life appears to be colourful and enriching. If we take a look into their lives we can find that they are always sought for advice not only in personal matters but also in official or professional matters. Such people always climb the ladder of success, simply because they know to communicate right things at the right place, in the right way at the right time.

Every individual has a sense of perception. When he looks at things in and around him it is quite natural that he perceives certain thoughts and ideas consciously or unconsciously. These ideas and thoughts get themselves stored in the subconscious mind. A person with a conscious mind tries to utilise these ideas in his day-to-day life, blending them with a variety of emotions and feelings. So, how effectively he applies his mood to blend various ideas and expresses them through language depicts the ability of that person to synthesise and integrate his head and heart to bring meanings to his life. Since these technocrats and Bschool pupils form the creamy layer of our society, it becomes inevitable on our part to groom them into powerful personalities. The best way to achieve such a means is to realise the fact that communication is not simply writing or speaking. It is rather a purposeful behaviour or an integral component of life, which contributes to an individual developing a remarkable personality as well as a distinctive inter-personal skill.

11

Academics of Teaching—Literary Theory and Practice

Nandini Sahu

> To teach is to be battered
> Scrutinised, and drained,
> Day after day. We know this.
> Still it is never said
>
> —*Jane Thompkins*

The art of teaching is an ego-battering exercise. Teaching, by its very nature, exposes the self to myriad forms of criticism and rejection, as well as to emulation, flattery, love, anger and every other human emotion and science, technology, theories and practice, every other human phenomenon. A ticking tenure clock, CD-ROMS, grade inflation, classroom preparation, presentation, use of audio-visual aids, explaining the toughest subjects in literature and technology—these all are only the externalisation of the personality and the psyche of the teacher. Knowledge, its utilisation, glorification of the personal as well as the academic skills, building the career and life of the pupils as a whole are the different factors that make a teacher's life successful. Also failure, panic, lack of preparation fraudulence, disorientation are some of the familiar themes of the academic version called teaching—the most challenging job. Richard Elmore, a professor at the Harvard Graduate School of Education writes, "teaching is a messy, indeterminate, inscrutable, often intimidating and highly uncertain task. Exposing one's knowledge, personality and ego to the regular scrutiny of others in public is not an easy work under the best of circumstances." As confronting a sceptical roomful of students every morning, getting drained out at the end of the day and being a matter of discussion at every dining table of the pupils with their parents, keeping pace between teaching and researchmay not always be a glad pursuit. Hence teaching is the most challenging, dynamic and the most demanding profession.

Before opting for teaching as a profession, one needs to have mastery over the subject and optimism towards life. Throughout the teaching career, the teacher needs to ask certain questions to himself: Is my life associated with my profession? Do I deserve to be doing it? Where am I going? Is teaching my passion? What will happen to me when I can no longer teach? These fundamental questions of identity and purpose are at the heart of literature as well. There are seven anxieties of teaching that are immediate, concrete and professional: lack of pedagogical training, isolation, stage fright, the conflict between teaching and research publications, course coverage, grading and peer evaluation.

Teaching is a demanding occupation, but few of us actually have studied how to do it. Most tenure professors at the beginning of the twenty first century picked up teaching through painful experience, doing onto others as was done onto them. Tales of initiation have a common narrative structure—how the novices stumble into their first classroom, do the best they can, and gradually find ways to overcome their fears of exposure and inadequacy, and shape a teaching style that seems congenial for their own personalities and environments. Jane Thompkins confessed in her book *A Life in School: What the Teacher Learned* (1996) that, "teaching was exactly like sex for me—something you were not supposed to talk about or focus on in any way, but that you were supposed to be able to do properly when the time came." Most teachers endlessly worry about what they are saying rather than what the students are learning. Sometimes the main points would get lost or squeezed into the last few minutes when the students collect their things, anxious about being late for the next class and no longer pay attention. Teaching preparation is a basic requirement for us. Every teacher should have well thumbed pedagogy books which provide an overview of research on learning in higher education, plus theories and techniques of course design, lecturing, leading discussions, giving examinations, grading, dealing with problematic students, counselling and handling cheating or plagiarism.

One of the best aspects of the work of teaching is that it doesn't have to be original to be good. We can borrow ideas and methods from our colleagues, predecessors, professors, we can imitate, copy and plunder in the confidence that the students will benefit from every good teaching technique we can put into action in our own classroom. As teachers we are not in competition with each other; teaching is not a zero-sum game, with the success of one subtracting form the failure of some other.

Teaching is perhaps the most privatised of all the public professions. Though we teach in front of the students, we almost always teach solo like a dramatic monologue, out of collegial sight— as contrast with surgeons or lawyers who work in the presence of others who know their craft well. When we walk into our workplace, the classroom, we close the door on our colleagues. However, if classroom teaching is private and isolated, lecturing is a public display of pedagogical techniques or their absence. That is why in many good universities of the world, beginning faculty participate in a term of workshops with other new teachers. The anxieties of isolation seem to be on the decline. Also, it is an opportunity for teachers to renew their own student roles, and to reflect on how they respond to various teaching styles. At the same time these teachers should have compelling enthusiasm and intellectual involvement. As audiences, they should not waste these occasions, letting the mind wander, applauding with polite imitation, and asking phony or competitive questions and finding ways to steer the conversation around to their own specialities and interests.

It is a matter of regret that many teachers believe that teaching versus research, and that for dedicated teachers there is hardly any time and opportunity left for research activities. On the contrary, we should research in ways that make our subjects more teachable, should reconceive our pedagogy to make it as intellectually challenging as our research reflecting upon our relationship between what we teach and how we teach in new ways, so that the same problems we deal with in our research including performance and narrative become a part of our pedagogical vocabulary. Teaching must become another subject of our research and publication.

Then, our internalised anxieties about the infinite amount of literary knowledge and the finite amount of academic time come together in worries about course coverage, performance appraisal and grading. One of the most difficult tasks for a teacher is deciding what to leave out. Instead of aiming for a comprehensive coverage of the syllabus, we have to think what the students need to read in order to establish a basis for further learning, and we have to adjust our intellectual aspirations to a realistic workload. Having struggled with textual triage, with deciding what is essential to what is inessential, we have to face the reality of standing up in front of a group to teach and its symptoms of stage fright and performance anxiety in front of all male and female students, sometimes with a body language of extreme resistance and hostility, folded arms, stony faces, occasional snickers and whispers. We can overcome this only with our radiating personality eclipsing theirs, becoming a role model for them.

Grading produces anxiety for teachers as well as students. Teachers can learn how to plan assignments and construct texts that match objectives to evaluation, and find ways to challenge students without giving in to ill-informed administrative pressure to fight grade inflation. One of the most persistent myths in academia is that the harsh and unpleasant, or mumbling and droning professor who never does well on evaluations is in fact the one the students will remember and cherish in years to come. About teachers who are tough, Walt Whitman writes, "Have you learned lessons only of those who admired you, and were tender with you, and stood aside for you? Have you not learned great lessons from those who braced themselves against you, and disputed the passage with you? Teaching is mysterious, and when the students are interested in the material, they will learn under any circumstances. Anyway, the tough drill-sergeant teacher or the talking-to-himself teacher is not a model to emulate.

Now to be specific about literature, teaching literature offers a teacher the best of all subjects to teach. In the past, most educators agreed that teaching literature was a way of making people better human beings. When English literature became a course of study in University College, London in the 1820's, its purpose was to moralise, civilise and humanise.

In the US, after the Civil War, literature was viewed as a repository of moral and spiritual values, bestowing a sense of national culture and heritage. To Yale's Williams Lyon Phelps, at the beginning of the twentieth century, "teaching was preaching about Christian values and moral uplift." Classical and modern literature was regarded as a quasi-religious repository of spiritual guidance. In the post-modern times, with our multidisciplinary approach towards science, technology and literature, the New Critical close reading isolates the litorary texts from historical contexts and subjective interpretation, and offe a toughrs mindod quasi-scientific methodology that give literary study some parity with the sciences as an academic discipline. Poetry, the favoured pedagogical genre of the new critics, has become a language laboratory of irony, tone, paradox and symbolism, and also an aesthetic sanctuary and harmonious retreat from social conflicts.

The teachers of literature testify the joy their work has brought to their lives. Leslie Fielder believes that "literature is for everyone— an introduction to works of imagination over which all human kind can weep, laugh, shudder, and be titillated, communal dreams, shared hallucinations, which in a time when everything else tends to divide us from each other, join us together, men and women, adults and children, educated and uneducated, black and white, yellow and brown, even teachers and students. In literature classes, when our objective is to introduce the students to the development of literary theories, our intention is to train our students to think, read, analyse and write like literary scholars to approach literary problems as trained specialists, to learn literary methodology, in short to "do" literature as scientists "do" science, and to do it through a hierarchy of cognitive skills: knowledge, comprehension, application, analysis, synthesis and evaluation. For instance, if we give the students the definition of iambic pentameter, discussing the theoretic part of the poem, as well as making them listen to the application of its sound pattern through audio-visual aids becomes a part of the syllabus. Thus, a theory class of elevated literature, accompanied by a language laboratory session compels our pupils to study literature as a craft rather than a body of isolated information, making them learn the following competencies and skills:

1. How to organise subtle and complex differences in language use.
2. How to read figurative language and distinguish between literal and metaphorical meaning.
3. How to seek out further knowledge about the literary work, its author, content, and interpretation.
4. How to detect the cultural assumptions underlying writings from a different time or society, and in the process to become aware of one's own cultural assumptions.
5. How to relate apparently disparate works to one another and to synthesise ideas that connect them into a tradition or a literary period.
6. How to use literary models as cultural differences, either to communicate with others or to clarify one's own ideas.
7. How to think creative about life by using as a broadening of one's own experience and practical knowledge.
8. How to read closely, with attention to detailed use of diction and syntax, metaphor and style, not only in high literary works but in decoding the stream of language everyone in modern society is exposed to.

9. How to create literary texts, whether imaginative or critical, making connection between literary works and life.
10. How to work and learn with others taking literature as a focus for discussion and analysis defending a critical judgement against the informed opinions of others.

The theory, perspective and frame of teaching creative writing is to make the pupils perceive, interpret and understand the world. The faculty effort is aimed at developing students' competencies and creative talents. Students' creativity should be inspired and colleges must add value by cultivating creative talent. James Duderstadt, President of the University of Michigan, noted that colleges, universities have focused on selection process in the recruitment of students and faculty and have given little or no attention to developing human potential and creativity. He has challenged the four traditional models of excellence in higher education—reputation, content, resources, outcome—and advocated a talent development model in which development of student and faculty talent should be primary specifically in the departments of creative writing. Teaching creative writing may be assumed to be a complex application of literary theories and research that requires considerable instructor training and continuous refinement of skills and procedures. Becoming a good teacher takes at least one lifetime of continuous effort to improve. "For things we have to learn before we can do them, we learn by doing them."—Aristotle.

Teaching dangerous subjects, black literature, any racial literature that may be biased, suicidal literature, death, murder, violence, sex, and some other human ambiguities can be explosive. The awareness the literature teachers bring to representations of race, dialect, and ethnicity does not usually extend to the many other difficult subjects literature presents, and sometimes romanticises, such as abortion, pornography, sexually graphic language, drug addiction, etc. The literature teachers should become accustomed to treating the material as functional or textual should overlook the sensitivity of content. One important principle is candor and clear labelling—telling students in advance that they may be offended or upset, conceptualising the topics with some sociological or historical background, being prepared for hyper reactive students and allowing opportunities for them to respond. Many important literary works deal with suicide—*Madame Bovary, Anna Karenina, The Awakening, The Bell Jar, Miss Julie,* and Shakespearean tragedies. Many writers like Hemmingway, Virginia Woolf, Sylvia Plath, Anne Sexton, John Berryman, John Keats, and Lord Byron were themselves suicidal. In an age when suicide rate had jumped dramatically, a story's glorification of suicide may pose special danger to students who fancy to romanticise themselves. Literature teachers can play a vital role in suicide, violence prevention for they are the first to recognise the psychic patters of the pupils. They valorise the rights of the traumatising pupils with their emotional and intellectual reactions and help them with their anxieties. Also many literature teachers find it awkward to discuss sexually explicit language in literature. Should the professor skip it in a lecture? Use euphemism? Condemn it? The professor's behaviour and tone are crucial in shaping a student's attitude towards sexual language. If he is embarrassed, they will be embarrassed. If he is salacious, they will leer. He should try to demystify and legitimize sexually explicit language in the classroom without using it in lectures, when reading passages from the text without fuss or emphasis. Teaching literature demands that we should rise to the occasion in the dark times, moments of collective or personal anguish. Literature professors have to think about the abstractions of professional ethics in a more urgent and existential way.

Teaching methods as a whole can be divided into three theories: subject-centred theories, teacher-centred theories, and student-centred theories. Subject-centred theories, which make teaching a political and intellectual conviction, emphasize on content and information. Teacher-centred theories make teaching a spiritual journey. Student-centred theories or teaching form the micro level focus on the way people learn, and the organisation of classroom process to maximise active learning. When a teacher desires to make his/her classroom teaching effective and memorable, he/she may emphasize on certain aspects like:

— a clear structure and outline
— a statement of objectives
— frequent signposts
— handouts, especially with spaces for students to answer questions, solve problems, or add their notes
— a shift of material and approach every fifteen minutes
— strategies for student participation— buzz groups, problem solving, and giving examples
— use of audio visual aids
— student votes on various positions

In our times, books, journals, websites provide detailed information about teaching, universities provide centres for teaching teachers, publish handbooks and newsletters, provide background resources, send consultants to visit the classroom and even to videotape it. Most academic departments have professors acknowledged to be outstanding teachers by both their peers and students. They have learnt to put together lectures that are both rigorous and stimulating; assignments are comprehensive, challenging, instructive and fair. They have found ways to motivate the students to want to learn, to coopt them into becoming active participants in the learning process, to help them develop critical and creative thinking and problem-solving abilities. The extensive researches regarding the interactive patterns of teaching suggest that cooperative learning between teachers and students produce greater achievement and higher level reasoning, more positive relationship among students, greater acceptance of differences, higher self-esteem, increased psychological health, and a number of other outcomes than do competition or working individualistically. In college teaching a paradigm shift is taking place. Minor modifications in current teaching practices will not solve the current problems with college instruction. Teaching success in today's world requires a new approach to instruction, which I have attempted to point out in the following table:

	Old Paradigm	*New Paradigm*
Knowledge	Transferred from faculty to students	Jointly constructed by faculty and students.
Students	Passive vessel to be filled by faculty's knowledge	Active constructor, discoverer, transformer of own knowledge.
Faculty Purpose	Classify and sort students	Develop students' competencies, talents and creativity.
Relationships	Impersonal relationships among students and between faculty and students	Personal transaction among students and between faculty and students.
Context	Competitive / Individualistic	Cooperative learning in classrooms and cooperative teams among faculty.
Assumption	Any expert can teach	Teaching is complex and requires considerable training at every step. The students should no more be socialised into a 'spectator' role, rather the teacher must get them to participate in the class.

The classroom is a microcosm of the world, dealing with every subject like literature, science, technology, biographies, natural history, Buddhist self-help books, *The Bible*, spiritual texts, mathematics, philosophy, travel literature, manuals of household, computing, geography, physiognomy, music. But teachers should be formal, objective in their approach to each subject, professionalism upholding the importance of the job over personal concerns. In spite of whatever feelings the teachers might be experiencing or distractions they might be facing those should always take a backseat to performance and the task at hand. Of course the teachers are not automations, and in various situations they need to give voice to the pain and suffering, to show the students that academic development is as much about sympathy, empathy and insight as it is about reason, hypothesis and deduction. When the teacher encounters a phenomenon as large as war, terror or violence, he can connect it to other parts of human experience. On the whole, teaching provides us with a depth of tragic understanding of life.

As there are hospitality rituals for beginning a class or a course, there should also be some for saying farewell. Whatever text we end with is an invitation to some kind of closure—apocalyptic, nihilistic, or comic. The final class should tally the score, review the semester's progress and the student's own development and, perhaps, return to the first class, hold the course up for the examination, give it a finish. The very final act is to break out of the frame, to direct attention to the next logical question, to leave the pupils in perplexity. In a away, the last class can attempt the rebirth of intellectual spirit that one hopes to encourage in students. In a real sense, teaching never ends and the conclusion of the semester does not conclude the teaching and teacher-student relationship. Stuart Sherman says, "a teacher's real influence may run long past the last encounter, even into later generations." In a Pueblo Indian poem, a teacher says in his last class:

> Hold onto what is good
>   Even if it is a handful of earth
> Hold onto what you believe in
>   Even if it is a tree which stands by itself
> Hold onto what you must do
>   Even if it is a long way form here
> Hold onto life
>   Even if it is easier to let go
> Hold onto my hand
>   Even if I have gone away from you.

Teaching offers the illusion of a fountain of youth. It brings us into contact with young people, their enthusiasm and freshness, and allows us to have an impact on their lives. Teaching is, after all, a work in progress as we age and mature, so too must we our teaching. Authentic teaching requires reflective practice. Both teachers and students have testified since time immemorial as to how the joy of teaching and learning has changed their lives, improved their future. The joys of teaching, the passion of making lives, surely predominates over every otherworldly phenomenon acknowledging the teachers as the real legislators of the world.

References

College English; Number-42, October 1990.

"Dream a Little Dream", *The Chronicle Review,* September 2001.

A Life in School: What the Teacher Learned, Jane Thompkins; Addison Wesley, 1996.

12

Linguistic, Science and Art of Language

S.K.Mishra

What is Linguistics?

The word linguistics originates from the Latin word 'lingua' which means 'tongue'. Linguistics must, therefore, certainly deal with language. This reminds me of the following quotation, I had come across when I had started studying linguistics: "The gift of language is the single human trait that marks us all genetically, setting us apart from the rest of life," Lewis Thomas, (*The Lives of a Cell*).

But before we actually begin to define linguistics, let us first understand what is NOT linguistics:

I. Linguistics is not a way to solve the problem of language users.

II. Linguistics is not an informal interest in language, however strong that interest may be.

III. Using a language is not linguistics, because using a language is not the same as studying a language. It is the objective study of language, and not the use of language.

IV. Linguistics is not an interest in language for some other purpose. It is an interest in language for studying language itself.

Now, by knowing what linguistics is not, we must be wondering what this excludes. As we can see, we started this topic with a question, what is linguistics? And we ended up with, what isn't linguistics? This was a deliberate action. As we can understand from the above discussion, it (linguistics) has something to do with 'language'.

One of the simplest definitions of linguistics is that it is a scientific study of language. David Crystal, in his encyclopedia, defines linguistics as a 'science of language'. It can also be defined as:

I. The scientific inquiry into human language—into its structure and usage and into the relationship between them (Finnegan & Besnier, 1989).

II. A scientific study of the systems/ principles underlying human language (Verma & Krishnaswamy, 1981).

As it is we can see that almost all definitions of linguistics emphasise three key words: Language, scientific, and study.

Hence, it is of utmost importance to know, first of all, what is language?

What is Language?

Animals, it is said, have a communication system as opposed to humans who have language. Language, in the restricted senses in which linguists coin the term, is a special gift to human beings. Only human beings have the gift of speech. The logical question therefore to ask at this point is, In what way does the human language differ as a means of communication from the system of animal communication? In order to answer this question we shall now read about the differences and similarities between human languages and natural animal communication system. These characteristics are set up (perhaps unfairly) in reference to human languages. Some of the important characteristic features of human languages are listed by Hackett which, when taken together, help us isolate language from other forms of communication. These are:

1. Duality of structure of patterning.
2. Creativity or productivity
3. Interchangeability.
4. Cultural transmission.
5. Displacement.
6. Specialisation.
7. Arbitrariness.
8. Redundancy.
9. Property of being dynamic.
10. Discreetness.
11. Reflexiveness.

We shall now examine these concepts in detail.

Duality of Structure or Patterning

Human language displays two levels of patterning: where meaningful units (i.e., phonemes) are combined to form arbitrary signs (i.e., words) and these signs in turn are recombined to form new meaningful larger units (i.e., sentences). In other words, in languages investigated so far two levels of structures are found: primary level compounding of sounds into words and secondary level, compounding of words into sentences.

Level-I :Compounding of sounds or phonemes

S + P + O + T = SPOT

T + O + P + S =TOPS

O + P + T + S =OPTS

P + O + T + S =POTS

Level-II :Compounding of words

He+opts+to+spot+the+tops+of+the+pots= He opts to spot the tops of the pots

There is no evidence of this type of patterning in any known animal communication system. Therefore, one can say that one major difference between human language and the animal communication system is the duality of structure present in human languages.

Creativity/Productivity

This feature refers to the fact that human language has the ability to produce new messages on any topic at any time. Human beings can create a sentence never heard of before. That is, the same limited sets of phonemes are combined in a novel form to give novel messages. For example, if I say, "Last night I had a pleasant meal with a leopard on top of a tree," it would be a novel sentence, which I don't think I have ever heard or read anywhere. The construction of such a sentence, therefore, involves creativity/productivity.

The following quotation sums up this feature of language: "The most striking aspect of linguistic competence is what one may call the 'Creativity of language', that is, the speaker's ability to produce new sentences, sentences that are immediately understood by other speakers although they bear no physical resemblance to sentences which are familiar (N.Chomsky).

Interchangeability

This feature means that all members (male or female) of the species can both send and receive messages. This is obviously true of human language. This is not the case with the animal communication system. Only foragers do bee-dance and only males perform birdsong. The calls are not interchangeable between the sexes in the animal communication system. But they are fully interchangeable in human language.

Cultural Transmission

Language is a set of conventions that have grown as a result of the common living of a large number of people. These are, therefore, conventions common to the entire social group, which uses the language. This implies that languages have to be learnt. They cannot be transmitted through heredity. Charles Hockett (1955) points out that the system of convention particular to each language is culturally transmitted (i.e., acquired through learning) and not genetically transmitted (i.e., acquired through heredity).

Psychologists often make a distinction between instinctive and non-instinctive behaviour. For example, human beings have no instinct about building houses. They have to learn how to build houses because nature has not supplied them with an inbuilt knowledge of engineering. Bees, on the other hands, can build beehives in hexagonal shapes without learning geometry. For them the knowledge about hexagonal shapes is inbuilt and genetically transmitted. We can therefore say that for bees making use of hexagons is instinctive, whereas for human beings, building a house is non-instinctive. This non-instinctive behaviour is acquired and hence human beings are able to speak many languages at the same time.

Displacement

Displacement implies that users of the system are able to refer to events remote in space and time. Animals cannot communicate about imaginary past or future which humans are able to do with language. In other words, animal communication is context bound but human language is context-free. Human beings can talk about experience without actually living them because human language is not controlled by stimulus.

Specialisation

This implies that there should not be a total physical involvement in the act of communication. Human beings can talk while engaged in activities totally unrelated to the subject under discussion. For example, they can talk about cricket while cutting vegetables. A bee in a bee dance, however, is completely involved physically in the communication process. At that point it cannot do anything else.

Arbitrariness

This feature implies that there is no natural or inherent

connection between a written word (or sounds) and its reference (or symbols). This is overwhelmingly true of human language with the possible exception of a few onomatopoeic terms. That is, the relationship between words and their meanings is quite arbitrary; it is a matter of conventions. For example, there is no logic behind why a word like rose refers to a flower and not to a horse or a cat or a pencil or a mouse! The decision that rose should refer to a flower of a specific kind is purely arbitrary. There is nothing specific about it. A few people decided to call it a rose and the society accepted it as a word of the English language. The animal communication system generally does not have any arbitrariness, although Vervet (a kind of a monkey) alarm calls are said to have arbitrariness.

Redundancy

There is a lot of redundancy in human language, for example, when we speak a sentence like: "Are you coming"? there are two markers to show that it is a question: (1) the placement of the helping verb at the beginning and (2) the rising tone with which the question should be asked.

And when we write the sentence there are also two markers to show that it is a question: (1) The placement of the helping verb at the beginning now (2) The punctuation (the use of question mark) at the end of the sentence to show that it is a question.

This kind of redundancy, i.e., two or three markers to show the same thing, does not exist in the animal communication system.

Discreteness

Bee dancing or bird-song seems to have very few discrete units, which are recombinable. Human language has phonemes, syllables, morphemes, and words, etc., which are discrete units and can be recombined to mean different things. That is, language consists of isolable, repeatable units. For example, with the help of three discrete units, p, a and t, we can create pat, tap and apt. This is not possible in the animal communication system.

Reflexiveness

By reflexiveness we mean the ability to use the communication system to discuss the system itself. No evidence exists that any other species writes grammar or linguistic textbooks.

So, by now we are in a position to understand several definitions of language that are available. A few are listed below:

I. Language is purely human and non-instinctive method of communicating ideas, emotions, and desires by means of a system of voluntarily produced symbols (*Spair,* 1921).

II. A language (is a) symbol system... based on pure or arbitrary convention... infinitely extendable and modifiable according to the changing needs and conditions of the speakers (*R.H. Robins,* 1964).

III. Human languages are unlimited... (an unlimited set of discrete signals)... have great structural complexity ... structured on at least two levels ... (the learning task is considerable)... are open ended... allow for the transmission of information (*R.W. Langacker,* 1967).

IV. When we study human language, we are approaching what some might call "human essence" the distinctive analytics of mind that are, so far as we know, unique to men (*N. Chomsky,* 1968).

Definitions are many and still it seems that every aspect of language has not been explored. So much has been said and yet so much has been left out.

Linguistics, A Science

Before starting a discussion like this let us have an idea as to what science is after all.

Many people think that the key thing about science is the subject matter, the things that scientists study. For such people, science is the study of the physical world of what it is made of (chemistry), the force and energy that operate in it (physics), living things (biology), stars and planets (astronomy) and so on. For them things that are not physical (the mind, emotion, human behaviour, art literature, etc.) cannot be part of science.

The other definition of science is that it seeks to explain why things are the way they are. It is the search for explanation, an attempt to answer the question, 'why' which is the essence of science. Science is about solving puzzles. And to solve a puzzle, you have to observe the facts closely, decide which facts are relevant and which are not, make imaginative guesses, and then check your guesses using rigorous logical thinking. A scientist, therefore:

A) believes that explanation is more important than just describing and classifying a wide range of data.

B) is willing to narrow the data and even put off for the time being problems, which could not be solved at the time.

C) uses abstraction and idealisation, and concepts and principles often remote from everyday experience, and

D) Recognises that being disproved does not devalue his/her contribution.

A linguist, just like a scientist, develops hypotheses, makes generalised statements and tests them against the fact of languages. And like scientific theories a linguistic theory has to not only explain the observed data but also predict that which constitute potential thought, not actual data. A linguist can make predictions about grammars and discoveries. And finally, like a true scientist, he is constantly engaged in discovering more about languages in refining his method of investigations and in constructing better theories. He also tries to find out linguistic universals.

Some of the methods of observation of a linguist include simple listening, phonetic transcription and the use of various instruments, such as oscillograph, soundspectograph, kymograph, chromograph, mingograph, larynogoscope, endoscope, sonograph, autophonoscope, breathing flask, strobolaryngoscope, electric vocal tract, pitch meter, intensity meter, speech stretcher, formant graphing machine, etc. Recorder and cassettes made in these ways help in various kinds of objective description. A linguist has a language laboratory too as a scientist, and nowadays computes have been made an integral part of this.

Finally, the closeness of linguists with other natural sciences like mathematics, physics, physiology, biology, zoology, etc., is another proof of this scientific nature. It touches on physics through acoustics, on physiology through the structure of the vocal organ, on zoology through the comparative study of the communicative systems of living beings. As mentioned by R.H. Robins, "Linguistics in its operations and statements is guided by three canons of science: (1) exhaustiveness, the adequate treatment of all the relevant materials, (2) consistency, the absence of contradiction between different parts of the total statement, and within the limits imposed by the two proceeding principles, and (3) economy, whereby other things being equal, a shorter statement or analysis employing fewer terms is to be preferred to one that is longer or more involved.

So, in a nutshell, it can be said that linguistics is a scientific study of languages. It may be inductive or deductive; it is, however, objective, precise, tentative and systematic. It is concerned with reportable facts, methods and principles. It works by means of observations, hypotheses, experiments and tests, postulates and inferences. It makes generalization and predictions; it formulates theories; its products are descriptive, verbal or algebraic statement about language.

Linguistics: the Architecture of Language

The great edifice or structure that the language is, it cannot be as it is without the art and architecture it has at present; and the architecture is nothing but the linguistics that has about such an architectural work high and grand like language. To put it differently, the speaker's knowledge of the structure of a language is his linguistic competence, and the way in which he uses it, is his linguistic performance. Whereas competence is a set of principles, which a speaker masters, performance is what a speaker does. The former is a kind of code; the latter is an act of encoding or decoding. As Chomsky puts it, "For any one concerned with intellectual processes, or with any question that goes beyond mere data arranging, it is the question of competence that is fundamental. Obviously one can find out-about competence only by studying performance; but this study must be carried out in devious and clever ways, if any serious result is to be obtained."

Competence in any sphere can be identified with capacity or ability, as apposed to actual performance. Competence in linguistics is the linguistic ability— the ability to produce and understand indefinitely many novel sentences. It refers to the native speaker's innate creativity and productivity implicit in the normal use of language. It is this linguistic competence, which constitutes the central subject matter of modern linguistics. In investigating linguistic competence linguists focus on the mental system, which allows one to form and interpret the words and sentences of one's language. The system is also known as the 'grammar' of that language. The major components of this grammar are as follows:

a. Phonetics – The articulation and perception of speech sounds.

b. Phonology – The patterning of speech sounds.

c. Morphology – The formation of words.

d. Syntax – The formation of phrases and sentences.

e. Semantics – The interpretation of words and sentences.

Hence, this is the architecture that we call linguistics that builds the structure of a language.

Different Approaches to Linguistics

a. *Traditional:* The traditionalists like Panini, Plato or Protagoras were interested in language as a tool for analysing reality. They believed that the structure of language was a product of reason. Linguistics was thus looked upon as subordinate to logic and philosophy and the linguistic description was prescriptive in nature. That is, they told people what they ought to use, following the great writers of that time, instead of describing what people actually use. This type of understanding and investigation of language continued until about the end of the nineteenth century.

b. *Structural:* This is a late nineteenth century phenomenon with the emergence of linguists like Ferdenand de Saussure (1857-1913) in Europe and Leonard Bloomfield (1887-1947) in America. As a reaction against the traditionalists and also because of the discovery of new languages, linguists of this period aimed at describing each language in its own term. Each language was treated with respect, which meant not trying to force it into the grammatical framework of any other language. Similarly, ideas regarding the superiority of the classical languages, and of the written form, were rejected. The colonial notion that the languages of the native people were primitive was thought against, because although many languages did not have a writing system, they were still highly complex and structured. Thus the emphasis shifted from the description of the written form of the language to the spoken form of the language. This resulted in treating language variety, dialects and registers as part of language; and because this spoken form became important, grammars proposed during this period became descriptive in nature as apposed to the prescriptive nature of traditional grammar. That is, grammar of the language now described what actually happened, what native speakers actually used instead of prescribing what people ought to see.

c. *Cognitive:* The latest phase in the development of linguistics started during the late 1950's when Chomsky published his syntactic structures. He rejected the structuralist view that the function of linguistics was simply to provide a classification and a terminology to talk about language. He argued that a linguistic theory must be able to capture the psychological aspect of the knowledge of language. That is, the human mind is not a blank slate. The aim of linguistics is to understand and explain the following.

    i. What is in the mind / brain of the speaker of English or any other language?
    ii. How did this knowledge arise in the mind/brain? How did we learn our native languages? Were we born with it? Or was it learned later? Or both?
    iii. How is this knowledge put to use in speech? etc.

For Chomsky, the business of linguistics was to construct a theory, which would explain and predict facts regarding languages. Chomsky has given a special name to this description: Generative Grammar or Transformational Generative Linguistics. Generative defines the aim, that is, the grammar should be able to generate all and only the correct sentences, transformational defines one of the means of achieving it. That is, a grammar which is able to generate all and only the correct sentences of the language by means of applying transformational rules is a Transformational Generative Grammar. Chomsky has, therefore, once more shifted the pendulum in the opposite direction by making linguistics a branch of cognitive psychology.

Hence, all these three approaches can be reproduced in a tabular form as described below:

Era	*Traditionalists*	*Structuralists*	*Cognitivists*
Name of Linguists	Plato, Aristotle, Patanjali,	Saussure, Humboldt,	Chomsky and Others.

(Contd...)

(Contd...)

	Katyayana, Panini, Dionysius, Thrax, Protagoras, Varoo, Quintillian, Donatus etc.	Hjelmslev, Boas, Sapir, Bloomfield, Whorf, Greenbery, Trubeztzkoy, Harris, Jackobson etc.	
Period	From 5th century BC to late 19th Century	From late 19th century to 1950's	From 1957 till now
Status of Linguistics	Linguistics was considered subordinate to logic & philosophy	Linguistics was treated as an autonomous science	Linguistics, a branch of cognitive psychology
Concept of Language learning	Did not talk about language learning	Behaviourists' view of language language learning	Cognitivists' view of Learning

Sociolinguistics

We can define sociolinguiestics as the study of language in relation to society. The question of who is a sociolinguist and who is not is not so important as the question of what the difference is between sociolinguistics and linguistics. A sociolinguist is interested in the functions of language and not just forms; communicative competence and not just linguistic competence. The basic concepts useful for the study of language in socio-cultured contexts, are speech community, speech repertoire, speech situation, speech event and speech act.

So, in a nutshell, an informal definition of socio-linguistics suggested by a linguist is that it is the study of:

"Who can say what, how, using what means, to whom and why".

Psycholinguistics

Psycholinguistics is a recent branch of linguistics developed in the sixties. It is the study of interrelationship of psychological and linguistic behaviour. It uses the linguistic concepts to describe psychological processes connected with the acquisition and use of language. Chomsky regards linguistics as a sub field of psychology, more specially, the cognitive psychology. This has opened new vistas in language acquisition. As against the behaviourist's argument, a mentalistic approach propounding innateness hypothesis in language acquisition in case of children was coined and this gradually gained ground. Though there still exists a difference between the empiricist's theory and mentalist's theory, it has been accepted that psychology does play an important role in language acquisition process, and 'psycholinguistics' therefore is a very important field of study.

Applied Linguistics

This can be described as the application of linguistic theories, methods and findings to the elucidation of language problems that have arisen in other domains. The term is especially used with reference to the field of foreign language learning and teaching, but it applies equally to several other fields, such as stylistics, lexicography, translation, and language planning, as well as to the clinical and educational fields like biological linguistics, computational linguistics, geographical linguistics, etc.

Applied linguistics is an interdisciplinary field as it draws upon related fields like psychology, sociology, pedagogy and linguistics in dealing with problems of language teaching/learning. The filed is practical in nature.

Scope of Applied Linguistics

A glance at the suggested areas in applied linguistics in the agenda of the Seventh World Congress of Applied Linguistics held in 1984 in Brussels clearly shows how different was the perception was in the mid-1980's. The Brussels congress suggested the following areas:

a. *Language problems in developing nations:* linguistic consequences of colonialism, national language problems, literacy programmes, etc.

b. Language and society (sociolinquistics)
c. Language and mind (psycholinguistics)
d. Language teaching and learning (foreign language and mother tongue)
e. Communication and interaction (discourse analysis, stylistics, translation, lexicography, etc)
f. Logico- linguistics (linguistic engineering, quantitative linguistics, logic, language, etc)

This gives an idea of the scope and domain of applied linguistics today.

Applied linguistics invites us to evolve a new kind of synthesis of disciplines that have been taken as clearly demarcated and well defined. The art of cooking, for example, involves several things; can we call this applied chemistry? First of all, cooking is an art as well as a science; secondly, it gets redefined according to the human situation in which it is practised. Similarly, applied linguistics is a new synthesis that should not be viewed in the light of the traditional motion of 'discipline'. It is rather multidisciplinary.

Before doing applied linguistics, it is good to understand, however, that it is unnecessary and even futile to define the scope of applied linguistics. The study of the relevance of language in all human activities and the problems arising out of such relevance is the pursuit of applied linguistics, and such a pursuit must necessarily be a cooperative venture.

Linguistics, An Indian Perspective

Sanskrit linguistics formally must have begun the day the Indian 'rishis' and 'munis' began to understand and interpret clearly the Vedic speech. The ancient Indians first turned to the study of their language for religious reasons to ensure that no corruption or modification should creep into thc sacred texts of the *Vedas* when they were sung and recited.

The *Rig Veda* says, every sound, the language originated from "Aum", the 'Shabdabrahma'. The *Rig Veda* is the oldest Hindu scripture dating back to 3000 B.C. It dedicates two entire hymns to speech (X.71& X.125). It mentions three-stages in the development of language: (1) inarticulate speech, (2) Primitive articulate speech and (3) Language proper. The inarticulate speech is the hissing of serpents, or the humming of insects, the notes of birds and sounds made by other animals. The primitive articulations of speech were first employed by men in imparting names to objects, thus leading to the third stage, that is language proper, which was created by wise as men cleanse cornflour in a cribble. (X.17.1).

Similarly, "Brahmanas", "Aranyakas" and "Samhitas" also deal at length with the language and its developments, syllables, interval between the syllables, etc. "Pratisakhyas" are the first treatises or phonetics and formal grammar. They provide a scientific classification of Sanskrit sounds and the 'ganas' (the list of words remarkable for grammaticality in any way). Yakshya's Nirukta of fifth century B.C. is another linguistic treatise that is preserved in India that offers some explanation on Vedic Sanskrit which is different form that of the *Upanishads*, the *Bhagavad Gita*, etc.

The linguists of the age are also many. Panini is the best known of the Indian linguists. His date is not certain but around 500 B.C. or later has been suggested in the light of the evidence available. Bloomfield has called Panini's grammar as "one of the greatest monuments of human intelligence". Its main characteristic is its startling economy and brevity. Other linguists like Katyayana in the post-Panini era, Patanjali (2nd century BC) and Kaiyyata are some of the names that did a splendid job in furthering Sanskrit's cause, and there was a virtual decline in linguistic research in India. Much later, Hemachandra (A.D. 1088 to 1172) did some significant work which is preserved in his creation 'Shabdanushasana".

It is a matter of credit that India's contribution to linguistics as a whole, particularly that of Sanskrit, has been greatly acknowledged by many Western scholars like

Bloomfield, William Jones, J.R.Firth, W.S. Allen, R.H.Robins, etc. William Jones even goes to the extent of saying that modern linguistics began in 1786 with the discovery of Sanskrit by the West, and he declared: "The Sanskrit language, whatever be its antiquity, is of wonderful structure, more perfect than Greek, more copious than Latin and more completely refined than either."

CONCLUSION

In spite of a lot of research and theories evolved thereby, linguistics is still evolving and perhaps the last words are yet to be told. Old theories are rendered null and void with new theories replacing them. New vistas are being explored and it is a real treat to watch that many linguists are in the job to venture into the unknown. Progress is the key word here with a hope of perfection that will soon follow.

13

Personality Development, Interpersonal and Communicative Skills

Sanchita Choudhury

Personality grooming is a basic and essential need of the hour. This is meant for one and all. Just like our daily course of staple food alone is not sufficient to give us the necessary nutrition to sustain and we need to take vitamins as supplements, similarly, to cope with today's competitive world and to be successful, traditional course of education needs to be supplemented with special training on personality development.

In order to sustain and succeed in this competitive world, the naive form of personality must be groomed well so as to make it fit for certain specific environment and purpose. In fact, personality is not merely a reflection of the outer self. In the words of Gordon Allport, it is the internal 'something' that directs and guides a person. It is therefore very essential to analyse the internal elements of a person.

This paper projects the need of personality development. However, it begins with the basic concepts on personality that common people bear in their mind, and how the psychologists have gone beyond the superficial level of common understanding. Apart from discussing the different theories of personality, its determinants and the ways of analysing personality, the paper also deals with the importance of honing the communicative and interpersonal skills, with a specific prescription for the technocrats. In the struggle for existence, only the fittest survives. And the challenge that today's technocrats face is no mean when compared to what their peers in other fields do. Budding technocrats of the present time must be in both the streams of 'learning' as well as 'grooming'. As such, the personality of the technocrats must be balanced, mature, attractive and strong enough to withstand and face the challenges.

Meaning of Personality

The word personality is not unfamiliar to any of us. Very often we come across statements like "O! Swami Vivekananda had a strong personality." Well, different people understand it in their own unique way. However, perceptions are similar but never the same.

The word personality has been derived from the Latin word *per sonare*. Originally it used to denote the masks worn by the theatrical players in ancient Greek dramas; gradually, the term came to encompass the actor's role as well. So, originally the concept of personality was related to a superficial social image that an individual adopted while playing life roles—a public personality. In this way, common people equate personality with physical attractiveness. However, a student of psychology may not agree to this layman's concept of personality, perceiving in terms of external appearance.

Even different psychologists have propounded different views on personality. According to Hilgard et al, "Personality may be understood as the characteristic patterns of behaviour and modes of thinking that determine a person's adjustment to the environment." Gordon Allport defines personality as what an individual really is, as an internal 'something' that steers, guides and directs all human activity. On the other hand, Carl Rogers views personality in terms of self, an organised, permanent, subjectively perceived entity, which is at the very heart of all our experiences. However, Sigmund Freud, a revolutionist in the field of psychology, describes the internal structure of personality. He says that it is composed of three elements:

the *id, ego, super ego.* In addition, some personality theorists emphasised the need to recognise the person-situation-interaction, that is, the social learning aspects of personality.

Actually, the concept of personality is very much subjective. The understanding differs from person to person. The more one delves deep in its ocean, the more one comes out with different streaks of light in terms of concepts. Some people feel that it is the characteristic patterns of behaviour and modes of thinking that determine a person's adjustment to the environment. There are others who feel that it can be described as how a person affects others, how one understands and views oneself, and one's pattern of inner and outer measurable traits. However, some people also feel that personality is the dynamic organisation within an individual of those psychological systems that determine one's unique adjustments to the environment.

Thus personality represents the sum total of several attributes, which manifest themselves in an individual. It is the ability of the individual to organise and integrate all the qualities so as to give meaning to life. Also, it is the uniqueness of the situation, which influences the behaviour of an individual. As such, personality in itself is a very diverse psychological concept.

Theories on Personality

Further, many theories have elaborated the nature of personality. Prominent among them are: (1) type theory (2) trait theory (3) psychoanalytic theory (4) social learning theory and (5) the humanistic approach. The type theory tries to classify personalities into distinct categories, whereas the trait theory essentially classifies personalities but based on measurable traits. The psychoanalytic theory is based on the in-depth study of individual personalities. Person-situation-interaction has been emphasized in the social learning theory. However, the humanistic approach is based on existential philosophy where human being is placed at the centre of everything.

Determinants of Personality

In fact there are several factors that contribute to give shape to personality. Some of the very important among them are heredity, environment, family, social and situational factors. And one can add many more to the list.

Regarding the complete development of personality all these factors do play their individual roles. However, the degree of their individual influence varies from person to person. And this is the reason why no two in this world are identical.

Stages of Personality Development

Now how personality gradually develops in a person, from the stage of infancy till the last phase of one's life (personality development is a continuous process), is indeed an interesting topic of study. Psychologists have come out with different stages in the development of personality.

Freudian Stages

Sigmund Freud has been the pioneer in terms of formulating a meaningful stage theory. He is the first psychologist to believe that childhood events may reflect on adult behaviour and consciousness. He has theorised that there are four universal stages of psychological development, which play a vital role in the shaping of personality: oral, anal, phallic and genital. Freud has included a period of latency, normally occurring between the ages of six or seven and the onset of puberty, in the overall scheme of development. But strictly speaking this is not a stage. The first three stages of development extend from birth to five years and are called pregenital stages, since the genital zones of the body have not attained a dominant role in personality formation. The fourth stage coincides with the attainment of puberty. The names of these stages are based on the regions of the body whose stimulation allows for the discharge of sexual energy, or libido.

However, many have criticised Freud's high reliance on sex to explain stages in personality development. Walter

Mischel says that without having at hand a suitable set of learning concepts and terms for personality development, Freud relied on his own preference for 'body language'. He has preferred to say 'anal' rather than 'development', 'oral' rather than 'compulsive', 'genital' instead of 'mature'.

Freud's Stages of Personality Development

Stage	*Age*	*Major Characteristics*
Oral	Birth to one year	Interest in oral gratification from sucking, eating, mouthing and biting
Anal	1 year to 3 years	Gratification from expelling and withholding feaces; coming to terms with society's controls relating to toilet training
Phallic	3 to 4 years	Interest in the genitals, coming to terms with Oedipal conflict, leading to identification with same-sex parent
Latency	4-6 years to adolescence	Sexual concerns largely unimportant
Genital	Adolescence to adulthood	Re-emergence of sexual interests and establishment of mature sexual relationship

Neo-Freudian Stage

Among the neo-Freudians Erik Erikson has given a new dimension to the development of personality, which he claims is nothing more than a systematic extension of Freud's psychosexual development. He feels that the social factors are much more stronger than the sexual factors. He believes that the social problems encountered in the course of development are more important stages in which the child faces a wider range of human relationships with its

Erikson's Eight Life Stages

Erikson's stages	*Age*	*Successes in meeting requirements of stage brings*	*Failure to meet requirements of stage brings*
1. Infancy	Birth to 1 year	Basic trust vs. pursuit of affection and gratification of needs, recognition	Mistrust Result of consistent abuse, neglect, deprivation of love, too early or hard weaning, artistic isolation
2. Early childhood	1 to 3 years	Autonomy vs child views selfs a person in his own right apart from parents, still dependent.	Shame and doubt Feels inadequate, doubts self, curtails learning basic skills like walking, talking, wants to 'hide' inadequacies
3. Play age	4 to 5 years	Initiatives vs lively imagination, rigorous reality testing, imitates, anticipates rallies	Guilt Lacks spontaneity, infantile jealousy. Suspicious, evasive role inhibition
4. School age	6 to 11 years	Industry vs has sense of duty and accomplishment, develops scholastic and social competencies, undertakes real tasks, put-fantasy and play in better perspective, learns world of tools, task identification	Inferiority Poor work habits, voids strong competition, feels mediocrity, lull before the storms of puberty, may conform as slavish behaviour, sense of futility.

5. Puberty & adolescence	12 to 20 years	Ego identity vs Temporal perspective. Self certain. Role experimenter. Apprenticeship, sexual polarisation, ideological commitment	Role confusion Time confusion, self-conscious, role fixation, work paralysis, bisexual confusion, value confusion
6. Young adulthood	20 to 24 years	Intimacy Vs Capacity to commit self to others. Attitude of care, respect and responsibility towards another	Isolation Avoids intimacy, feelings of social emptiness and isolation. Seeks interpersonal encounters which are purely formal (employer – employee). Insulates himself against any type of real involvement. Attitudes of futility and alienation regarding his vocations.
7. Middle adulthood	25 to 65 years	Generative Vs Productive and creative for self and others, parental pride and pleasure, mature, enriches life, establishes and guides to next generation.	Stagnation Egocentric, unproductive, early invalidism, excessive self-love, personal impoverishment, self-indulgence, feeling of hopelessness and meaninglessness
8. Late adulthood	Old age (Suns years)	Integrity Vs Appreciates continuity of past, present & future, fully satisfied. Death not feared, 'wisdom of old age' comes into being.	Despair Time is too short, finds no meaning in life, has lost faith in self and others, wants second chance at lifecycle with more advantages, fears death. Often senile, depressed spiteful and paranoid.

maturity. In order to develop a healthy personality, psycho-social crisis during the different stages of one's life should be optimally resolved.

Cognitive Stages

Jean Piget, a Swiss psychologist, has talked about 'cognitive' or 'conscious' stages of personality development. For Piaget, it is the 'conscious' instincts, which are important variables in the development of personality. Piaget has spent most of his time studying child psychology (when and how children develop the reasoning abilities). He has identified four stages of personality development as shown in the table below.

Stage	*Age*
Sensorimotor	0 –2
Preoperational	2 –7
Concrete operational	7 –11
Formal operational	11 & above

By sensorimotor, Piget means that the infant responds to stimuli quite directly with little on the way of complex information processing. During the preoperational stage, the child learns to separate itself from the environment and initially classify objects (the first origin of analytic capacity) through the use of symbols and words. The concrete operational stage is characterised by an intellectual understanding of the concept of conservation of a mass, irrespective of its shape. In the final stage, the formal operational stage, reasoning takes place on abstract as well as concrete levels.

Immaturity to Maturity

Prof Chris Argyris of Harvard has identified specific dimension of human personality as it develops. He proposes that human personality progresses along a continuum from infancy to the state of maturity rather than going through distinct stages. However, at any stage, people can have their degree of development plotted according to the seven dimensions shown in the following table:

The Immaturity to Maturity Continuum

Immaturity Characteristics	*Maturity Characteristics*
Passivity	Activity
Dependence	Independence
Limited ways of behaving	Diverse behaviour
Shallow interests	Deep interests
Short-time perspective	Long-time perspective
Subordinate position	Superordinate position
Lack of self-awareness	Self-awareness and control

Argyris argues that healthy individuals tend to move from immaturity to maturity. That is how a person transcends from the ground level of immaturity to the level of maturity.

Ways of Assessing Personality

The need for measuring personality of people is imbued with multiplicity of justifications. The understanding of personality greatly influences several decisions like hiring personnel, establishing relationship, designing motivational packages in the organisations, etc. In fact, before the grooming process starts, it is essential to know and identify the behavioural traits of a person. However, at present there are many ways of assessing a person, which may vary from time to time, and situation to situation, depending on the purpose of its assessment.

The three widely used methods of personality assessment are:

1) Personality Inventories
2) Projective Tests
3) Assessment Centre

Personality Inventories

This is the most widely used method of personality assessment. This method consists of a number of statements

('Personality Inventories') relating to a specific dimension of personality of the individual. These statements become the basis for prediction and understanding of personality. The individual is asked to indicate his/her degree of agreement or disagreement with regard to each statement.

Projective Tests

Projective tests are basically designed to know the more subtle aspects of personality. Accordingly, these tests are based on the basic underlying assumptions that measuring some of one's dormant feelings, aspirations, ambitions, and hopes can assess one's personality. Inkblot Test, Thematic Appreciation Test (TAT), Sentence Completion Test, World Association Test, Picture Frustration Test are some of the projective tests to name.

Assessment Centre

The concept of an assessment centre was initially applied to military situations in the German army in 1930s. To assess candidates in a social situation was the basic purpose here. This concept travelled from army to the business world during the 1960s. The various simulated exercises are used here to evaluate personality which include situational tests, management problems, in-basket exercises, business plan presentations, situation decision making exercises, and so on. The multiple trained assessors observe the participants' behaviour and rate them based on predetermined dimensions, considered crucial in their work.

Myers-Briggs Framework is a popular questionnaire with 100 items, and is widely used to understand personalities. Based on the classical work of Carl Jung, the Myers-Briggs Type Indicator (MBTI) asks people how they usually feel or act in a particular situation. Again, based on the answers received, people are differentiated in terms of four general dimensions: sensing, intuiting, judging, and perceiving. Higher and lower positions in each of the dimensions are used to classify people into 16 different person categories. The MBTI is indeed a popular instrument used to assess personality types. It is widely used in the selection process.

The Big Five Model illustrates the five personality traits. The 'Big Five' framework continues to attract the attention of both researchers and managers. The potential value of this framework lies in the fact that it encompasses an integrated set of traits that appears to be valid predictors of certain behaviours in certain situations. This is primarily based on research conducted in the United States of America.

Now, once the traits and types are identified in a person, personality grooming must start hitting the targeted areas, especially the Achilles' heel. However, personality development, or in other words personality grooming remains incomplete if the inter-personal skills and communicative skills are overlooked.

When we point out a person with strong and attractive personality, we actually mean the person's magnetic traits in personality. And it is never without his proficiency in inter-personal and communicative skills. That is, the grooming and developmental process remains incomplete without these two. For example, relationships based on talent and personality alone, without character is like good looks without goodness. The bottom line is that a lasting winning combination requires both character and charisma.

Personality Grooming and Technocrats

Keeping in view all these factors, it may be inferred that along with the development of personality, the process of grooming is very essential to get a deserved reflection by exploiting the external factors to the most. Deliberate and rigorous grooming is undoubtedly a process to chisel an uncut-gem-personality in its crude form. If this deliberate process of grooming is not implemented on a person, then its development process will be exposed to almost all the factors, which may interfere in an unorganised way and clash with each other. Hence the result may not be socially accepted. As such, to see a balanced and successful person of tomorrow this training process of grooming personality must start from the very tender stage of infancy.

In today's competitive world, life is full of uninterrupted challenges. To face, tame and win over them is no child's play. But actual difficulty crops up while accepting failures. Seldom do people accept and introspect their failures. So, herein the training of personality grooming plays the real role. So, personality grooming not only helps one reach the goal and succeed but also helps maintain it. It is a must for those who dream to fructify it; those who like to be the fittest among the survivals.

Technocrats are not away from the world. They are among the creamy layers in the society. Obviously, they face more challenges than the common mass. Hence, for them this special grooming process must start right from the beginning of their professional career. In order to achieve professional success, this training or grooming process is inevitable. Care must also be taken to develop the communicative and inter-personal skills for complete personality development. However, it is only possible if the professional institutes encourage this so that the budding technocrats get trained and groomed by the well-trained professionals.

Interpersonal Skills

Here are some of the factors, if kept in mind, help develop interpersonal relationships.

1. Being good to others. "When you are good to others you are best to yourself".—Benjamin Franklin.
2. Life is a boomerang. So one should treat people with respect on the way up because there is a chance of meeting them on the way down.
3. One should see the things they are and not the way one is.
4. Trust is very important here. Relationships fail to bloom if there is no mutual trust.
5. The factors that prevent building and maintaining positive relationships must be kept far away and beyond one's reach. These are:

— Selfishness
— Self-centredness
— Lack of courtesy
— Inconsiderate behaviour
— Not meeting commitments
— Rude behaviour
— Lack of integrity and honesty
— Arrogance and anger
— Conceit
— Negative attitude
— Closed mind
— Aversion to listen to others
— Suspicious nature
— Lack of respect for values
— Lack of discipline
— Lack of compassion
— Impatience
— Manipulative behaviour
— Escapist behaviour
— Touchy nature
— Inconsistency
— Unwillingness to accept truth
— An uncaring attitude
— Greed. It is like seawater: The more one drinks, the thirstier one gets.

This probably is not an all-inclusive list. Most of us may have some of the characteristics mentioned above. Some may have more than the other. The objective is to evaluate and adjust the course in those areas.

6. Ego conflict is a big hurdle on the to develop healthy relationship. Knute Rockne says, "Egotism is the anaesthetic that deadens the pain of stupidity."

7. One should have an open mind instead of an empty mind. An open mind is always flexible; it evaluates and may accept or reject ideas and concepts based on merit. An empty mind is a dumping ground for good and bad. It accepts without evaluation.

Communicative Skills

Personality development remains incomplete if the communicative skills are ignored. For a technocrat this is very important to master to reach the pinnacle of success. In fact many problems generate due to poor communication. So, it is very important to identify and avoid the communication barriers (mainly psychological, semantic and physical).

Some knowledge on modern grammar is very essential to speak and write flawless English (English is the *lingua franca* in India as well as in many parts of the world). Pronunciation with correct accent and stress increases the degree of understandability. Words should be dealt with proper care lest they should not change the meaning. This is again possible if the professional institutes encourage in establishing language laboratories. Students will then get exposed to many software tools (language modification tools, language correction tools, phonetics recognition tools, etc.) to train themselves and know their shortcomings and strong points. For the overall development of personality it is very essential. However the guides also play a crucial role here, by taking individual care and giving them the best polish to shine forever.

Steps to Build Positive Personality

Accepting Responsibility

When people accept additional responsibility they are actually giving themselves a promotion.

Responsible behaviour is to accept accountability and that represents maturity. Acceptance of responsibility is our attitude and the environment we operate in. It should be inculcated right from childhood. It cannot be taught without a certain degree of obedience.

2. Consideration
3. Think Win/Win
4. Words should be chosen carefully before spoken.
5. One should minimise criticising others. Positive criticism is rather a better alternative.
6. Smile is a magic wand
7. One should put positive interpretation on other peoples' behaviour.
8. One should be a good listener.
9. One should be enthusiastic.
10. One should give honest and sincere appreciation.
11. One should accept mistakes willingly.
12. 'Be grateful but do not expect gratitude'. This should be one's attitude.
13. It is better to forget than forgive. As such one should avoid bearing grudges.
14. Confidence without humility is arrogance. Humility is the foundation of all virtues.
15. To have a friend be a friend.
16. One should not be sarcastic and put others down.
17. A sense of humour does magic.
18. One should be understanding and caring.
19. One should practise courtesy on a daily basis.
20. Sympathy is, "I understand how you feel" and empathy is, "I feel how you feel." So, it is better to show empathy than mere sympathy.

Personality Development

How personality should be developed in a person has been exhaustively explained in the *Bhagavad Gita* too (chapter 13, shlokas 7 to 11, as told by Lord Krishna). Human being is a social animal. So, a person whose personality has not been groomed in accordance with the society, may find himself unfit to survive. In fact most of the problems crop up because of the lacunae in personality.

Human beings create their own problems. So, they must find a solution too. Personality must be groomed from the tender age. But one can never interfere with the elements descended from forefathers through genes. However, it is only through the deliberate grooming process that one can project or suppress them. As such to build a world free from hatred, jealousy, violence, intolerance, envy and many more negative forces, is not impossible at all. If we take collective responsibility to be good human being, then more than half of the job will be done.

"Svi:ya a:ra:dhana—sarva a:darana" (worship one—respect all) should be the ultimate goal in this entire personality building process.

References

1. Cattell, R.B., "Personality Pinned Down", *Psychology Today*, July 1973.
2. Ruch, Floyd L., *Psychology and Life,* Chicago: Scott Foreman, 1963, p.353.
3. Allport, Gordon W., *Personality—A Psychological Interpretation*.
4. Aswathappa. K., *Organisational Behaviour,* Mumbai: Himalaya Publishing House, 1991.
5. Khanka. S.S, *Organizational Behaviour*, New Delhi: S.Chand, 2000.
6. Robins, Stephan P., *Organizational Behaviour*, New Delhi: Prentice-Hall of India.
7. www.charminghealth.com
8. www.chinnayeeyar.org

14

Influence of Situational Factors on Communication in the Practical Life of Engineers

Atish Chandra Sarkar

Everybody accepts the fact that communication is an important tool in the practical and professional life of engineers. All technocrats use communication, in its various forms, in the day-to-day life – be it in the industries, be it in the research laboratories or be it in technical education. Parallel to their knowledge on the technical matters, engineers in the field of sales, marketing, business development, projects, production and maintenance need to have good communication skills to be successful in professional life. Essentially all of them are required to work in teams where mutual coordination, comprehension and communication are some of the basic requirements of the job.

Importance of Learning English Language

Today there is no denying the fact that language teaching is important in the technical education. In India, English is the lingua franca. English is being taught in our country from the school level and by the time students reach the graduate schools for technical education, they are already equipped with the basic knowledge on this language, its grammar and other common usages. But English is a foreign language. So a commonly observed phenomenon with many Indians is that while they communicate in English, a process of direct translation from their respective mother tongue language goes on at the back end of the brain. As a result, often we hear wrong usage of English that could be easily traced back to the corresponding vernacular use of the same. It is clearly evident from the following example when somebody says, "Listen, listen boys, the matter is urgent" (a direct translation for, "Suno suno larkon, yeh mamla bahut jaroori hai"). Therefore, learning correct English, free from the influence of the vernacular languages, is very important. Erudite technocrats at senior official positions may face embarrassment due to their wrong English.

Role of Engineers

Now, let us see the evolution of roles in the career of engineers. Engineers join industries as technical hands. Gradually with time, they become managers as their responsibilities increase in the managerial field. Finally, an engineer is required to perform as a leader. So in this process of transformation, a technocrat is required to work with people, understand and develop interpersonal skills, build relationship and network with people in various hierarchical positions, social stature and intellectual levels. Engineers also need to command and motivate a team of people having diverse background and qualifications. Needless to say here that whatever be one's technical skills, without a command over communication and human skills, success is likely to remain an unachieved dream in life.

Handling Real-Life Situations

So, when the necessity of communication skill is well understood, let us deliberate on how in real life, different situations cast spells on the effectiveness of communication. Engineers do communicate in the day-to-day life in industries through various modes – verbal, written, electronic signals, audio-visual, etc. Now, how, do the situations influence effectiveness of communication in real life?

A person may have a good communication skill – does that essentially mean a sure success for him in his career? Probably the answer is 'no'. Here we would discuss the influence of situation on people – how human beings, while communicating, get diverted from the focus under pressure, miss important points in a stressed condition or leave communication halfway through during a crisis period while thinking it to be complete.

To elaborate the situational influence on communication, let us see the following case study. At the end of it, we would probe into what actually went wrong with the protagonist in the case study.

Case Study

Amit did his graduation from a reputed engineering college in computer science. He is technically sound, smart and hard working. He has an admirable command over communication skills. He gives good oral presentations and speaks correct and fluent English.

For the last four years, Amit has been working in a top-notch IT company. Presently, he is a Group Leader, working on a project for developing automation solution for a multinational bank. His Reporting Officer is his Project Leader who is also the boss of four other Group Leaders like Amit. A team comprising five junior Programmers work under Amit.

Amit's Project Leader would be making a presentation in the corporate office tomorrow. For this, Amit and his boss worked till very late last night. They prepared their presentation in the Main Hall's stand-alone PC where usually all the presentations are conducted in this office with the help of an attached LCD machine. They completed their worked yesterday and made a rehearsal before calling it a day.

Today as Amit arrived in his office at 9 in the morning, his first job was to copy the presentation material on a CD and hand it over to the Corporate Group because his Project Leader had taken a one-day leave today. Amit switched on the PC in the Main Hall. But the PC started getting hung every time. After a few trials, Amit rushed to the phone and called the maintenance group to check the machine. Amit said on the phone,"...please do something – we have to give a presentation. It is urgent." He had just kept the phone on the cradle when it started ringing. He forgot that he had an appointment with his customer's representative at 9:30 to discuss about some banking process details related to his project. The representative was waiting for Amit at the Reception in the Ground Floor.

Amit was about to leave for the Reception when Mr. Das, Private Secretary to General Manager, appeared in his cabin and informed him that some of GM's guests would be visiting their office premises at 10 am. The visitors car number was OR –16 W2122. The GM had requested Amit to arrange an Entry Pass for the visitors, as they did not have any valid pass to enter the premises.

Now Amit had many jobs to attend to simultaneously. As he looked outside, he found the maintenance group entering the Main Hall. He was relieved to some extent. As he was moving downstairs to meet the customer, he saw Pranay, his peer and another Group Leader in his project. He immediately said to Pranay, "Hi! Please do me a favour. Some visitors will be coming at 10. Please hand over this Car Entry Pass to the gatekeeper at the Main Gate before 10." Pranay nodded and took the pass from Amit and went away.

Pranay went straight to the Main Gate and handed over the pass to the keeper there with a one-line message," Allow the car inside when it comes." The gatekeeper saluted Pranay and kept the pass in his pocket.

At 10:05 a.m. Amit was on his way back to the Main Hall after finishing his meeting with the customer. In the lift, he met Pranay and confirmed the matter on the entry pass again with him. But there was shocking news waiting for him as he reached the Main Hall. A peon intimated the message left by the maintenance group for him that the presentation could be started anytime now as the maintenance people, being unable to fix the problem, provided another CPU and took away the existing one for repair. Amit could feel a chilling sensation in his spine, as he knew with that old CPU, their entire presentation matter was gone. How to manage the corporate presentation then? He felt at a loss as there was no time left for handing over the CD to the Corporate Group.

It was around that time (10:35 to be precise), Mr. Das, PS to GM, again came to Amit's cabin. This time in a stern voice, Das informed him that the GM's special guests were held up at the main gate for the last half an hour and it was purely Amit's failure to get them in. Amit was not at all prepared for this. He started sweating and became immensely tensed, as he could not understand what had gone wrong at the gate.

Now let us see what had actually happened at the Main Gate. Everyday, schedule change of gatekeepers' duty takes place at 10 a.m. This point was missed by both Amit and Pranay. The visitor's car came a little late at 10:15. Before it arrived, the change of duty occurred. But the last keeper forgot to pass on the Car Entry Pass to the next gatekeeper and he went away with the pass still in his pocket.

Amit, sitting nervously in his cabin, was busy framing reasons and explanations on how to handle the situation and face the bosses. He was anticipating a call from the GM's office anytime. At 11:10, a phone call really came asking him to see the GM at once. Amit could hear his own heartbeats as he rushed to the GM's office.

As he entered the GM's cabin, Amit found the senior boss was sitting in front of two outsiders (who appeared like suppliers). The GM said straightway, "Amit, have you finished the job I gave you last week, preparing the inventory of spares required in your project – PCs, cables and other network devices? These gentlemen have come to check the list – bring it right away."

Now, Amit was not at all prepared for such a question, and at the back of the mind as he started to recollect about the list of spares, he remembered that he had left the job half done owing to other important jobs in hand. But at that moment, when his mind was already preoccupied with many other things, he could not even gather the right words to explain the matter to the GM. And the smart boy Amit, started sweating profusely while searching for words and ended up stammering and fumbling. Thus he presented a very poor profile of his own in front of his superior and outsiders.

Analysis of the Case Study

What was the root cause of Amit's failure – what went wrong with Amit? If we analyse correctly, we would find the following communication failures in it that in turn complicated the situation and led Amit to such a miserable plight.

i) When Amit rang up the maintenance group, he did not give them a complete picture of his problem. He talked about a technical problem for which he, being a technical person himself, always sought a technical solution. But the way he stated his problem ("...please do something – we have to do a presentation. It is urgent"), he could not anticipate that other people might solve it managerially by replacing the CPU which would definitely not serve his purpose. Actually he should have elaborated his real problem that he needed to make a copy on a CD from its hard disc. So one root cause was very poor and half-hearted communication by Amit to the maintenance group.

ii) When Amit requested Pranay to hand over the visitor's pass, it was a casual communication that he did. ("Hi! Please do me a favour. Some visitors will be coming at 10. Please hand over this Car Entry Pass to the gatekeeper at the Main Gate before 10.") Though his communication was otherwise complete yet he failed to put stress that these visitors were guests of no less than the GM. He did not give sufficient emphasis to make Pranay understand the importance of the visitors who in turn did the same casual approach while communicating to the gatekeeper. And definitely no manager (like Amit) could justify his failure by stating it to be a gatekeeper's mistake.

iii) In the office of GM, Amit, in spite of being a smart presenter, presented himself in a very poor manner, which might have created a bad impression. And in real life, such impressions do matter a lot while the performance of a person is judged or evaluated. And today Amit definitely could not do justice with his ability and potential because of the pressure factor and the tensed situation through which he was passing.

Situational Factors in Real Life

From the above case, we understand that having good communication skills is not enough to be successful in real life. It is a fact that many good communicators fail in real life because of poor application. In real life, the situational pressure makes all the difference, which is absent in an ideal situation that exists in a classroom.

Engineers in the practical life are often exposed to situations that may have one or more of the following characteristics:

a) Working under time constraint
b) Working under resource constraint
c) Doing many jobs simultaneously
d) Planning for many jobs for concurrent execution
e) Putting one's brain in more than one critical thing
f) Fulfilling orders / requests of several bosses
g) Being under pressure due to the high risk involved in the job
h) Feeling tensed due to apprehension of the cost of failure
i) Fearing one's own reputation at stake
j) Handling machine breakdowns
k) Handling emergency / contingency situations like fire, gas leakage, power failure, etc.

Recommendations for Effective Communication in Any Situation

To be successful in the real life, one needs to eliminate the situational factors that might influence the effectiveness in communication. For this, a certain amount of exposure to the crisis might help the students. In technical colleges, during the academic sessions, communication skills may be developed by practising under simulated crisis situations and /or by analysis of real-life case studies.

The following guidelines may be useful during any communication:

To overcome the Situational Factors

a) Remain cool and composed in crisis.

b) Try to have a bird's-eye view of the entire situation.

c) Try to think that nothing is at stake even if something goes wrong.

d) Draw a sequential chart in the brain for the jobs at hand.

e) Prioritise the jobs—discriminate the urgent jobs from the important jobs.

f) Apply reasoning and analytical power and avoid being too much involved emotionally.

g) Speak clearly and boldly while communicating (see some tips at 'A' and 'B' below for two different target groups).

'A' —Verbal Communication to Subordinates / Peers

a) Know who the target audience is.

b) Estimate (roughly) the background, ability and intellectual level of the audience.

c) Anticipate what the audience is expecting and what they might overlook or miss.

d) Be brief and to the point.

e) Get rid of mental preoccupations, if any, during communication.

f) Repeat the key points.

g) Cross check by taking response / feedback.

'B' — Verbal Communication to Superiors

a) Anticipate the mood of the boss.

b) Anticipate what the boss is expecting.

c) Be courteous.

d) Be brief and to the point – do not waste the boss's time.

e) Use chosen / premeditated / selected words.

f) Be attentive.

g) Avoid overdoing anything to create impression.

Conclusion

Developing communication skill is not an end in itself. It is just a means. Its analogy can be drawn with learning to how to drive a car. To learn driving is not sufficient, but one needs to drive the car safely to reach the goal every time, in time, whatever be the traffic condition or condition of the roads. Similarly, in order to be effective and successful in real life, communication skills need to be applied properly and relentlessly—day in and day out—to overcome the effects of the situational factors.

15

Importance of Language Studies in Technical Education

Sanjeev Kumar Pattnaik

Personality development and interpersonal skills plays a very vital role in each and every aspect of our life, whether it is personal or professional. Or in other words, it is a prerequisite for success. And for this success communicative skill plays an important role. Effective communication is a short-cut to distinction. This communication gives us an edge over others. It is this communication which makes people successful and brings them to the limelight. We talk of any group of people or from any profession. It is mainly the communication which has given them the distinct edge, whether it a successful businessman, or a politician or the babas or any other person.

So far as you are concerned, the young technical minds of today, tell me one thing—are you any way different from a person doing the same engineering degree from anywhere in India, or do the companies in the job advertisement ever mention any specification that any person who has passed his degree only from Bangalore or Mumbai or any other specific place can apply? No. Which means that even the companies do not discriminate. So any person whose level of preparedness and competence is on par with the requirement of the company gets through.

In order to prove the level of preparedness we need to have among various other attributes, qualities and skills, communication as the *bramhastra*, which will help us to fight the Mahabharata of the highly competitive world. Communication plays a very vital role in each and every aspect of our life. It is how we speak or communicate which is more important than any other thing. Communication influences, motivates, intoxicates and convinces people to our way of thinking.

This is the primary and the most important tool to be a leader.

If communication is not effective or there is a barrier, it amounts to disaster, where the intensity is much more than the World Trade Tower disaster.

Hence, to avoid these kinds of disasters language studies plays quite a distinct role in technical education and the use of linguistic software is definitely going to enhance and enrich the quality of preparedness and competence in the budding technical professionals who are molding themselves to face the tough competitive job market. These software really blends the young technical minds with personality development and interpersonal skills. But certain points are to be borne in mind that firstly it should be palatable to each and every student and reach out to every student. Secondly, it should not confine itself only to some few, rather it should cater to the needs of all the students at the same time.

Remember that it is small things in life which matter the most and hurt the most—like, we can sit on a mountain and enjoy the serenity but we cannot on a pin. Similarly, in technical education communication is most neglected, as it is considered to be a very small thing, but when a person stumbles in the professional career because of this small thing, it not only hurts but pains. It is absolutely suicidal to ignore communication in technical education. People may be technically strong but unless they communicate it is of no use, it is just a waste. So professional success depends on 22 per cent of technical skills and 78 per cent of soft skills, the major skills being communication. Even the corporate look for people who have a perfect blend of knowledge and soft skill. At Wipro, of the total allocated to training budget 40 per cent is for soft skills enhancement. Why is that in an organisation like Wipro they need soft skills training? Because success means analysing and upgrading. To go up the ladder we need soft skills—the major being communication. Hence, if knowledge is food for life, communication is salt, and attitude adds flavours.

A perfect blend of knowledge, skills and attitude is surely going to take you to the pinnacle of success.

16

Importance of English Language for the Personality Development of Technical Students

Jayashree Nanda

Human beings have a distinctive characteristic of communication through language. Language is an important vehicle by which society is structured, and the culture of the race is transmitted from generation to generation. A child learns the language of his society. The process of interaction through language shapes his personality with the other members of his environment.

Language is not a natural phenomenon; it is a creation of man's social needs. Hence, human beings depend on language, as they depend on air, water, and the earth around it for their own existence. Language is an extremely complex and highly versatile code that is used to communicate our thoughts, desires and experiences to other persons. Language and human culture are intimately related and the one is indispensable to the other. When man's attention is turning increasingly towards analysing his culture, it is natural that he should attempt to examine in detail the means of communication, which is essential to his society. Language, like society, is constantly evolving and is subject to growth and change, in much the same way as a living organism.

Language has always had a place in human affairs. One of the greatest achievements of man is his ability to use language. Language in fact is a great tool, which has made human civilisation possible. Language is also the most important tool for thinking.

IMPORTANCE OF ENGLISH LANGUAGE

English occupies a prominent place in the association of languages that have flourished so far. It is the queen of languages. Though it is originally the mother tongue of Britishers, it is now the mother tongue of the people of so many countries of the world. English is said to be a foreign language.

If it is a foreign language why should our children learn this language? What is its importance and place in technical education?

An International Language

English is one of the most widely spoken languages in the world. It is the means of communication between people of different countries. One person out of every ten in the world speaks English naturally. It is the language of international politics, trade, commerce and industry. English is one of the six official languages of the United Nations. As an international language English has created better understanding among the nations of the world and has been responsible for cultural give and take. It has facilitated mobility of teachers and students from one country to another. Thus it has also created worldwide scope for employment.

A Link Language

English is the only language which is understood by the educated people all over the country. The trade correspondence from one state to another is mostly conducted in English. In the absence of English, a person from Mysore will not be able to communicate with a person from Orissa, nor can a Marathi share his thoughts with a Punjabi. Thus English is a unifying factor and helps national integration. The correspondence between the union government and the state government is mostly conducted in English.

(III) A Window on the World

English is a language, which serves as a window through which the light of scientific and technological development of the world, and the explosion of knowledge, pour into the countries of the globe. It is a pipeline for the stream of knowledge in all branches of learning. The Radhakrishnan University Education Commission observed, "it (English) is a language, which is rich in literature – humanistic, scientific and technical". If under sentimental urges we give up English, we will cut ourselves off from the living stream of ever growing knowledge. In fact, it will not be wrong to say that English is a window through which we are able to see the scientific, technological, agricultural, commercial and literary developments, taking place in the world. F.G. French has rightly pointed out that anyone who can read English can keep in touch with the whole world, without leaving his own house.

A Library Language

English is the key to the storehouse of knowledge. Even though some universities have switched over to regional languages as media of instruction in humanities it will take some time to extend this step to courses in science, law, medicines, engineering agriculture. The Kothari Commission has rightly emphasised that English would play a vital role in higher education as an important library language. The commission has said that no student should be considered as qualified for a degree, in particular, a master's degree, unless he has acquired a reasonable proficiency in English. According to this, the implications of this (English as a library language) are twofold: (i) all teachers in higher education should be essentially bilingual. They should be able to teach in the regional language as well as in English. (ii) All students and particularly postgraduate students should be able to follow lecturers and use reading materials in the regional languages as well as in English.

The Official Language

English is the official language of the central government and some state governments. Although Hindi is the official language used in central administration, English is still used in all administrative and judicial matters. Similarly, although regional languages are used as official languages in different states, English has its own place in all administrative matters.

From the above discussion, it becomes clear that English helps us keep in touch with the world's ever-increasing explosion of knowledge and technological advancement, which is an important factor for a developing country like India. If we just look up at space technology, we can find that without adequate knowledge of English, we cannot understand and absorb the developments in the field. Any attempt of translating technical terms into regional languages will be disastrous and will have an adverse effect on the Indian space programme, which will come to a standstill in the absence of English-educated scientists, technicians and engineers.

For bringing about revolutionary changes in various fields such as agriculture, medicine, industry, transport, telecommunication, etc., it is essential for us to be in touch with the outside world and it is possible only with an adequate knowledge of English. It is only through English we can bring various scientific discoveries to our country.

For us Indians, English has a special place. This is not merely because English is a world language, but because it also has historical associations and has made an impact on our cultural life. For this reason, English is not a foreign language to us, it is a second language. So in the teaching of English in India we should treat it as a second language and not as a foreign language.

The place of English in present-day curriculum clearly indicates the absence of a uniform policy. A quick step must be taken to give English its appropriate place. We should lay much emphasis on our mother tongue and at the same time English should be added in our curriculum. It should be simple and utilitarian. In teaching English to our students, our aim should be to enable them to use English with ease and comfort, that is, to use it both instrumentally and integratively. That is to say, they should be able to speak and write English effectively and develop an ability to understand the basic patterns of culture of the English-speaking people.

English is very rich in scientific and technical knowledge, and so the knowledge of English is the only means of preventing our isolation from the world. Discarding English will amount to closing a window on the world of technology. We will fall back by hundreds of years and will never be able to catch up with the developed world. We cannot think of taking India into the twenty first century without capitalising on English. The study of English will continue in our country for the progress of the country.

Our country is rich in natural resources but the people are perishing in poverty. Explosion of population, unemployment and burning food problems are standing in the way of our prosperity. Our nation needs scientific and technological knowledge for the betterment of our people. This knowledge can be had through this international language, i.e., English. Our future citizens of the nation need to be trained in technological 'known-how'. This purpose can be achieved if they learn English.

Role of English Language for the Development

1. Development of self-confidence.
2. Development of interpersonal relations.
3. Development of self-concept
4. Identification with conditions and characters in the larger world.
5. Increased ability to generalise the facts
6. Increased ability to understanding
7. Increased ability to deal with abstraction
8. Development of imagination

9. Ability of problem solving
10. Increased ability to communicate with other persons.
11. Ability to make decisions
12. Understanding of moral concepts
13. Development of leadership qualities
14. Development of team spirit.
15. Increased ability of making adjustments to situations and individuals.

In conclusion, one fact may be stressed again. Our world and society are changing very rapidly. Contemporary civilisation is moving quickly due to vast technological advancement, and we cannot say what situations the next generation will have to meet and what problems they will have to face. The pattern of life will not continue to be the same, and therefore, education should make them good and effective problem solvers, teach them habits of creative and critical thinking, cultivate among them attitudes of rapid reorientations in the face of new situations, and develop among them intellectual resourcefulness. Therefore, our children should be imparted this language to enable them to acquire the skill of the same, so that they can become true citizens of India and genuine inhabitants of the world. They can bring peace and prosperity, both to the motherland and Mother Earth, 'the globe'. For this English language will stand as the green signal of liberty, equality, tranquillity and tranquility of the world for ages to come.

References

A.L. Kohli, *Techniques of Teaching English*, 1970.

C. Paul Verghese, *Teaching English as a Second Language*, 1989.

N.P. Pahuja, *Teaching of English,* 1995.

S. Venkateswaran, *Principles of Teaching English*, 1995.

S.R. Sharma, *Teaching and Development of English*, 1993.

Lecturers in Education, Kunja Bihari College, Barang, Khurda.

17

Role of Discourse Analysis in Second Language Teaching and Learning

Kunjaban Patel

Though Second Language Teaching (SLT) in the last few years has already undergone several revolutions, we, the English teachers in India, do not seem to be aware of such revolutionary changes, what to speak of applying those new ideas in the Second Language Classroom (SLCs), we continue to teach in a social vacuum. Hence, even after several years of serious and sincere teaching, the Second Language Learners (SLLs) fall to communicate in real-life discourse situations. The result is either break of communication or miscommunication, which instead of solving problems often create new ones at the social and cultural levels.

In a multilingual country like India, English is the lingua franca through which future citizens, who are being groomed in the second language classrooms, are going to discuss and sort out the problems of the society. The teachers of English must not, therefore, forget the vital role they are going to play in helping learners master the English language. The second language learners should, therefore, not only be taught the linguistic aspect of a particular utterance but they should, rather must, also be made to realise the social significance of such an utterance in the ongoing discourse.

Discourse analysis addresses itself precisely to this task as well as to the solving of social problems arising out of such linguistic miscommunications and breaks of communication. Second language classrooms, in order to be really useful to the society, must, therefore, incorporate in itself the insights of the researchers in the field of discourse analysis.

In a multilingual and multi-cultural country like India English as the common second language has a very crucial role to play in establishing communication among inter-lingual speech communities. It also means that the teachers of English have now to play a much more important role than they used to play traditionally. The traditional emphasis on teaching the use of correct grammatical sentences has proved a failure since it could not provide the learners any discourse competence. That is to say, learners no doubt could produce isolated grammatically correct sentences, but they could hardly produce chunks of language which might be called a coherent piece of discourse. Hence, the current thrust on shifting the emphasis from teaching sentences to teaching discourse. But, we feel, even that is not enough. English teaching, in order to be really effective in the Indian setting, must also incorporate in its linguistic content the insights provided by cross-cultural and cross-linguistic discourse analyses.

A discourse analysis approach views language as a dynamic, open system by means of which members of a speech community exchange information, maintain social relationship and contribute to the culture of that particular community. That is, language, like other socio-cultural elements, has not only structural regularities but also regularities of usage. It is a vehicle for conveying not simply information in communication but also self-expression in terms of motives, emotions, desire, knowledge, attitudes, and values.

Discourse analysis has come of age in the last two decades and has already built for itself a significant foundation in the areas of both descriptive and applied linguistics. The various disciplines like linguistics, sociology, psychology and anthropology which feed into discourse analysis have contributed towards its development as a broad-based discipline sharing a common interest in language in use, that is, in real people using real language as opposed to studying artificially-created sentences or chunks of language.

The term discourse analysis is used here to mean the linguistic or sociolinguistic analysis of naturally occurring discourse or text, spoken or written, the minimal length of such an instance being two utterances or two sentences.

The direct applications of discourse analysis – which have now gained currency as Applied Discourse Analysis – to language teaching, mean several things. Some of these are: teaching language as communication (Widdowson 1978: Brumfit and Johnson, eds., 1979), communicative syllabuses rather than grammatical syllabuses (Munby 1978), teaching English for science and technology (EST) or for other academic purposes (EAP) or teaching English for special purposes (ESP). Applied linguistics has to recognise that language is studied for different reasons. Often the study is instrumental, a means to an end and not an end in itself. The concept of notional or functional syllabus is an instance of such a use of language as an instrument. It holds that the syllabus can be constructed round a list of speech acts, communicative and semantic categories. This would be radically different from the traditional grammatical organisation of most syllabuses. We are, however, concerned here with the insights of discourse analysis which, we feel, have a direct bearing on the linguistic input, both in terms of quality and quantity, in the second language classroom.

Since language is the central means by which people communicate with one another in everyday life, understanding communication is an important goal of linguistics. The way we communicate is a part of our cultural repertoire for making sense of – and interacting with – the world. In other words, our linguistic behaviour is affected by, and is an integral part of, the culture we belong to. Cultures differ greatly in their value systems, customs and beliefs, behaviours and lifestyles. Accordingly, the linguistic behaviour of people representing these cultures as well as those of different speech communities vary greatly. A cultural frame of reference, therefore, becomes increasingly important when the distance is greater between languages. But a cultural perspective is needed even with nearby languages in order to grasp the social significance of a linguistic feature, such as terms of address, politeness formulae, conversational openings, turn-takings, closings—including silence—and the accompanying paralinguistic features like nodding, bending, hand movements, tone of voice, pitch, loudness, pause, etc.

Language as an offshoot of culture manifests in itself certain features of the culture it represents. There are underlying cultural value systems, which play a crucial role in determining discourse production and comprehension. They also affect the ways a particular language is used by its speakers in their day-to-day intercourse with others within the same cultural group. Their worldview, day-to-day lifestyle, beliefs, customs, social and moral values – all influence their use of language. That is, the native language of the speaker reflects the cultural features of both the community and the individual himself. The cultural features are so deeply amalgamated in the linguistic behaviour of the speaker that even when he uses a second language some of these features, if not all, come up on the surface of the second language. Hence, the need for the inclusion of cross-cultural and cross-linguistic features in the study of English, the commonly shared second language of the Indians.

We must bear in mind that there are a lot of verbal and non-verbal differences involved in cross-cultural communication that can cause misunderstanding, failure and distrust in communication. Thus, the meanings of verbal and non-verbal signs have to be matched according to the situation, and the social and cultural background. In order to reduce the risks of 'culture shock' and communication breakdown one has to become fully aware of differing ways of behaviour, particularly the linguistic behaviour, of the interactants. As mentioned earlier, one has to learn about the day-to-day lifestyle, beliefs, customs, and social values of the speech community or culture groups one is interacting with or likely to interact with. These cultural indexes become no less significant even when the two different speech communities are using a shared common language—'English' in our case.

Today learning a common second language in such a diverse culture as ours, therefore, means learning a great deal about the culture of the speech communities one is likely to interact with. We may cite one or two examples in this connection. In many cultures of India wives do not take the names of their husbands. This affects their address system where taking the names of husbands is involved. In certain cultures of South India marital relations between an uncle and his maternal niece is considered sacred whereas in many parts of India such a relation is a taboo. Such a diverse change of relations also gets reflected in the address system of these cultures.

We may mention here one more commonplace example which the teacher can easily exploit to show the differing ways of behaviour on a particular occasion by learners representing diverse socio-cultural backgrounds. We know that people greet one another in several ways. For the sake of convenience let us divide them into three groups — (a), (b) and (c). Learners belonging to group (a) Greet one another with folded hands; those of group (b) by touching the feet of the elders, and those of group (c) by shaking hands. What is of relevance to us here is that such differing ways of greeting also get reflected in the linguistic system of the interactants. We know that touching someone's feet means showing a much greater degree of reverence than greeting with folded hands or shaking hands. Consequently, the linguistic system of group (b) will definitely have a more elaborate system of politeness and honorific markers than the linguistic system of groups (a) and (c). In a situation where an elder member of group (b) is greeted with folded hands or with a handshake, he will, in all likelihood, get a shock and consider such a thing not only impolite but downright insult. But if a learner is already made aware of such a diverse system of greeting, he will very likely change his way of greeting accepting this as part of the diversity of our culture and social system.

We may say that once such an awareness is developed in the learners they would easily accept such sociolinguistic diversities as part of the cultural mosaic of our country, and would gladly sort out any possible future problems arising out of any miscommunications. In the language classroom also there would be less of teacher dominated talk and more of learner-dominated talk by adopting the method of role-playing as suggested above. Classroom discourse could also be used both as input and as output to the learning process by providing a two-way information flow rather than a one-way flow of teacher-dominated talk. The second language classroom, in order to be really effective, needs to change itself from being teacher-oriented to being learner-oriented.

What all these mean is that the second language teacher or the English teacher has also to perform his new role as a cultural 'go-between' in addition to his already important role as a language teacher. All these will also bring about a change in the nature of the second language classroom.

Language classroom – any classroom for that matter – in India do not any more consist of monolithic groups either linguistically or culturally – except maybe in remote corners. It, in a way, helps the language teacher. He can now easily draw upon the native recourses of his learners in order to show cultural and linguistic diversities in the performance of different speech acts such as addressing, requesting, opening and closing a conversation, being polite, etc., and also to show how different cultures (such as 'nodding' in South India which might be taken as 'no' instead of 'yes' by people of many other parts of India). Such an exercise would not only develop an understanding of one another's culture but also help remove a great deal of possible miscommunications or breaks of communication. Such an exercise would also make the language class highly interesting and qualitatively rich.

As far as the quantitative aspect is concerned, we should see to it that the language classroom becomes more learner-dominated and not teacher-dominated, as has been the tradition. The teacher should relegate his own 'all-knowing' posture to the background and take a heuristic role monitoring the whole procedure than dictating terms in the classroom. This would facilitate quicker and better learning through interactions among the learners than in the conventional one-way manner.

In fact, Clyne (1994) points out, "there is now a greater need for studies in cross-cultural setting. An increased range of data would facilitate the establishing of parameters, the separation of the relative from the absolute, and their development of a culturally neutral mode of description."

As we have been arguing, the second language classroom, in additional to its being a language learning classroom, should also become a cultural training centre so that it will inculcate in the learners an understanding and respect for one another's culture. This is particularly relevant in a multi-lingual and multicultural country such as ours. It also calls for discourse studies in cross-cultural settings so that syllabus designers can fruitfully use the insights of such studies in designing second language syllabus to make it socially relevant for the future generations.

Bibliography

Apte, M.L., 'Language in the Socio-Cultural Context' in Asher (1994) (pp.2000-10), 1994.

Asher, R.E (Ed.), *The Encyclopaedia of Language and Linguistics*, Vol. II, Pergannon Press, Oxford, 1994.

Blum-Kulka S, House J, Kasper G (Ed.), *Cross-Cultural Pragmatics.* Ablex, Norwood, NJ, 1989.

Brumfit, C.J and Johnson, K., (Eds.), *The Communicative Approach to Language Teaching.* O.U.P., London, 1979.

Crystal, D., *Cambridge Encyclopaedia of Language.* Cambridge University Press, 1985.

Garcia O, Otheguy R (eds.), *English Across Cultures: Cultures Across English*, Mouton de Gruyter, Berlin, 1989.

James, Carl et al., *Cross–Cultural Correspondence : Letters of application,* C.L.C.S Occasional Paper No.38, 1994.

Kachru, B.B., (Ed.), *The Other Tongue: English Across Cultures*, University of Illinois Press, Urbana, 1982.

Munby, J., *Communicative Syllabus Design.* C.U.P., London, 1978.

Price, J. (ed.), *Cross-Cultural Encounters*, River Seine, Melbourne, 1985.

Stubbs, M., 'Applied Discourse Analysis and Educational Linguistics' in *Applied Linguistics* Academic Press, London, 1984.

Thomas, J., 'Cross-Cultural Pragmatic Failure', in *Applied Linguistics* 4.3. pp. 91-112, 1983.

Van Dijk, T.A. (Ed.), Handbook of Discourse Analysis, Vol.IV: *Discourse Analysis in Society.* Academic Press, 1985.

Widdowson, H.G., *Teaching Language As Communication*, O.U.P, London, 1978.

Wierzbicka, A., *Cross-Cultural Pragmatics.* Mouton de Gruyter, Berlin, 1991.

Wilkins, D. A., *Notional Syllabuses,* Oxford University Press, Oxford, 1996.

18

Why's and How's of Intercultural Communication

Tripti Mund

Intercultural communication is the process of communication between the people of different cultures, where the degree of misinterpretation is greater as compared to that of communication within a culture. As we know, a complete circle of communication is a six-phase process:

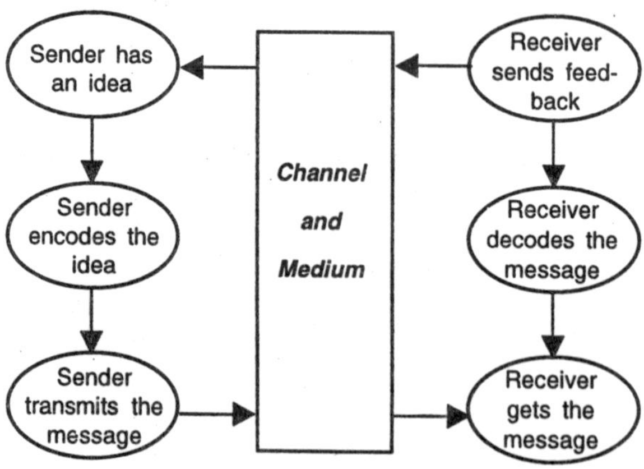

Sender to receiver and then back to the sender. It seems smooth but that is not all. Communication depends on what verbal and non-verbal signs the sender sends and how the receiver interprets these signs. In intercultural communication the cultural differences tend towards the misinterpretation of sent signals. Until a decade ago intercultural communication was not viewed with much importance. But market globalisation and its resultant multicultural workforce has necessitated intercultural communication.

Market globalisation is to view all the markets of the world as a unified whole. It is not a new phenomenon. Professor Theodore Levitt of Harvard Business School first used the word. The process started in the 1880s with Ford, Singer, Gillette, National Cash Register, Otis and Western Electronics globalising their economy, but in the process paralysed in the inter-war period. The renaissance of globalisation began about three decades ago with the technological advances in transport and communication.

The revolutions in technology like fax machines, overnight delivery of services, email and the internet has globally increased the potential of even small firms. Those who could not even think of trading beyond their city now becamo traders of international repute. Globalisation made it easy to penetrate into the geographic and economic borders of others. Companies had to cross the cultural borders to be successful in foreign lands.

Globalisation and international mergers led to immigration and emigration, which brought together varied languages and cultures to a single workplace. Globalisation or glocalisation both have the similar challenge of interacting with people of different national, religious and ethnic groups. Cultural diversity in workplaces has forced to think on effective modes of intercultural communication.

The business firms need to focus on intercultural communication. The reason is business messages need to be conceived and planned in the readers point of view. The US, for example, has 65 per cent of multicultural workforce with people from Latin America, Canada, India, Africa and Asia. This percentage is expected to rise in coming the decades. Why only US, India too is rapidly expanding in its multicultural workforce, especially with the IT giants

Infosys, Satyam and Wipro. A diverse workforce brings with it a wide range of skills, tradition, backgrounds, experience, outlooks and attitudes towards work. This poses a greater challenge for the employer to communicate with and motivate these diverse employees. For example, it would be difficult to motivate a typical Indian woman to wear an above-knee skirt to her workplace. She may feel it vulgar but for an American it is her usual formal wear.

In today's scenario one of the roots of success is to be sensitive to the intercultural differences. We belong to several cultures. In the micro-perspective each individual has his own cultural identity which is communicated through the coordination of his body language and his manner of speaking. An individual identity always has the reflection of his own culture in the city or country to which he belongs.

Culture as a whole is the shared system of symbols, beliefs, attitudes, values, expectations, and norms for behaviour. Apart form the culture of his country a person belongs to the culture of his workplace. Each profession has its own register and customs abiding that register. In the social perspective cultural norms are taught right from the childhood of how and what to think and act. The rest is acquired through experience and observation.

Each culture has its predefined thought processes, behaviour, and communicative methods. For example, an ideal Indian family comprises a man's parents, brother, and sister along with his wife and children. He ought to satisfy the needs of each individual. But in the US the situation may differ. His family may only comprise his wife and children. Culture is also a hereditary phenomenon that passes on from person to person and from generation to generation. But the following generations are not the carbon copy of the previous. They are highly vulnerable to additions and deletions. Take the example of the outfit of Indian youth of this generation.

One of the important ways to improve intercultural sensitivity is to recognise cultural differences. In a multicultural workfield a person, can be an effective communicator only if he is able to overcome his ethnocentrism.

Thus intercultural communication can complete its cycle if the sender first decades, then recovers cultural cocoon and sends his message according to the receiver's culture. That is, he can be effective only if he can recognise the cultural differences. For instance, one should avoid presenting a green-coloured object to a Chinese or a Malaysian as it connotes illness and death. Symbols also need to be interpreted correctly. Seven, for instance, signifies good luck in the US and India too but it is just the opposite in China, Ghana, and Kenya. It is the common practice of the people to treat others the way they wanted to be treated.

One can improve intercultural sensitivity by recognising and accommodating the cultural differences like contextual differences, legal and ethical, educational, social, aesthetic, materialistic, non-verbal differences cues, and environmental stimuli to understand the meaning of a message sent by a person of the same culture. But this meaning may range from culture to culture. If the cultural context is divided into high–context and low-context culture, it is observed that high context people rely more on non-verbal actions and low-context people on verbal communication. Non-verbal actions include the related environment of gesture. And tone modulation, which is not taught but is learnt by South Koreans and Chinese, are all high-context culture people. But the Americans and the Germans who come under the low context culture spell out their rules and expectations through statements, like, "Please bear with us" or " You are most welcome."

The decisions, problem-solving techniques and negotiating styles all depend on the cultural context of the person. Low context culture by to reach decision quickly and efficiently. Thus the U.S. business people enjoy debate and confrontation but the Japanese avoid it as it may lead to a conflict.

The legal binding of a high-context culture is more flexible than that of a low-context culture. Every business firm has to operate within the jurisdiction of a legal system. And the legal systems vary from culture to culture. In English common law that is followed by US, UK and Canada someone is presumed innocent until proved guilty. But in Nepolionic Code of Mexico and Turkey someone is presumed guilty until he is proved innocent. To extend a business into another culture or to immigrate to another country for job procreation one needs to be acquainted with the legal proceedings of the country.

For successful business proceedings the ethics of that region has to be understood. For example, it is unethical in the US to take bribes but in Kenya it is part of life. It is not possible for any business firm to understand the legal and ethical procedures of another culture in detail. The legal and ethical biases can be avoided by:

— Flexible and mutual acceptance of another's culture.
— Trusting the values of each other.
— Being honest and sending correct messages.
— Respecting cultural differences.

Every culture has a set of rules that may be formal or informal. Formal do's and don't's are well defined and taught right from one's childhood. But the informal set is difficult to be distinguished as it may undergo numerous permutations depending on the environment and the individual. Like the traditional Indian table manners are completely different from that of the Western culture. We also have set rules for how men and women should or should not behave. Aesthetic perception, education, religion and superstition, attitudes and values, material culture all play an equal role in the making of the social culture.

Aesthetics pertains to a cultural sense of beauty and good taste, and is expressed in arts drama, music, folklore, dance and the like. It is of special interest to the business executives as these govern the norms of beauty in a society, and are helpful in correctly interpreting meanings of various methods of artistic expressions, colours, shapes, forms and symbols in a particular culture. For instance, black is the colour of mourning in the US whereas white in most Eastern countries. Sensitivity to the aesthetics of a society and their symbolic expressions can greatly help in avoiding socially embarrassing situations and correctly designing the products and messages.

Education is important as it affects not only the educational level but also the mental development and various skills. In general, educated people are more sophisticated, discriminating and receptive to new products and ideas. Availability of educated manpower is dependent on a country's educational level.

Religion and superstition are the major determinants of moral and ethical values, and influence people's attitudes, habits and outlook on life that are reflected in their work habits and consumption patterns. Dr. Earnest Dichter has observed, "In puritanical cultures, it is customary to think of cleanliness as being next to godliness. But in catholic and Latin American countries, to fool too much with one's body, to overindulge in bathing or toiletries has the opposite meanings. It is that type of behaviour which is considered immoral." To show respect to an individual, one can address someone as Mr. John, Ms. Jenny in the US but in China it should be according to the position one holds.

The Americans are highly materialistic people. They spend more time in earning money as they feel it is the sign of superiority. Thus they work for 300 hours more than the west Germans and 60 hours more than their Japanese peers.

Non-verbal communication makes it easy to derive meaning, provided the communicators are from the same cultural background. Even a simple hand movement of a person of one culture can be different for another. In intercultural communication, space and gesture are the two elements of non-verbal communication that are to be considered.

Space determines the comfort zone between one person and another. In Canada and the US people stand at least five feet away during business conversation. Arabs love to come close. But for a German or Japanese the five feet gap is offensively too close.

Gesture makes it easier to grab the meaning of confusing messages. But cultural differences mean differences in body language too. Hence during intercultural communication there is every change that a person may misinterpret and misunderstand the other's body language. A person mastered in another's spoken and written language may not know the nuances of another person's body language. For instance, people in the US and Canada shake their heads back and forth to say no; in Bulgaria it is nodding up and down; in Japan it is moving your right hand and people in some societies raise their chin. Gestures cannot be taught easily, but for improving intercultural sensitivity one has to recognise the cultural differences of the other country.

Ethnocentrism is another attitude that creates misinterpretation and misunderstanding in intercultural communication. The best possible way to avoid it is to talk to Mr. Reddy as Mr. Reddy and not as the stereotype of the Telugus as a whole. One should avoid the stereotyped image formed for another culture. Of course it helps in the initial stages of understanding a culture but it may not help although, like a Japanese visitor may stereotype Americans as people who walk fast, are wasteful in utilising space, speak directly, ask too many. Questions and are undisciplined. But this may not hold true when he is talking to Mr.Bob Crew. One can overcome ethnocentrism by:

— Recognising the cultural differences between others and yours.

— Avoiding assumption that a person is a stereotype of his culture.

— Respecting others' culture.

Overcoming Communication Barriers between Cultures

After recognising what makes a person of one culture different in his communication skills with a person coming from another culture, let us focus on how one can effectively develop the art to communicate interculturally.

- To send intercultural messages effectively one has to study the other cultures. Spending sufficient time with them is the best method to study other cultures. But it is not always practicable. So to know the depths of other cultures one has to read books and articles on the culture. Reading should include the culture's history, religion, politics, values and customs. Also one should talk to people who have already done business with that culture. A minor mistake can be misinterpreted and one may even pay to the extent of losing one's business. Like a decent handshake with a Spanish must have five to seven strokes, for a French a single stroke is enough. A successful businessman always remembers to follow these tips.
- To assume differences until similarity is proved.
- To initiate communication.
- To improve his habit of listening patiently.
- To make complete use of his body language to show respect to the other cultures.
- To communicate from the receiver's point of view.
- To learn the art of tolerating a misunderstood or ambiguous statement.
- To don't form impressions through dress or appearance.
- To identify his own cultural bias.
- To be flexible in adjusting with other cultures.
- To emphasize the similarities between both cultures.
- To communicate with the individual and not the stereotype.
- To be situational in direct communication.
- To access feedback provided by the recipient.

Each profession has a register and thus a culture of its own. UK and US are two English-speaking countries but at several instances their registers follow different words for the same thing. For example, in the US it is an apartment for a flat in UK and elevator for a lift in UK. The US-UK language barrier is not a difficult one but one has to really work hard to break the barriers of language where English is spoken as a second language.

In an interaction between English speakers and ESL speakers misunderstandings are mostly due to the vocabulary and pronunciation. The ESL person tends to bring in his mother-tongue words and accent into his English. The less fluent ESL persons have every chance of missing out information, as they are more acquainted with the formed methods and not the slangs and typical idioms of the US or the UK English. Thus to break the barriers of ESL remember to:

— Avoid using slang and idioms.

— Pay attention to local accents and pronunciation, like it is difficult for the Americans to pronounce French 'r' or the German 'ch'.

— Be aware of vocal variations like tone modulations. Russians speak in a flat, level tone that bores the US listeners.

— Respect preferences for communication styles. US workers are direct and straightforward in their style which may not be accepted by the Japanese and Chinese who go for indirect and roundabout polite approach.

With globalisation English has become the official language for communication. Look at the recruitment websites of any non-English-speaking country and you can find apart from other recruitment, fluency in English is highlighted. With increasing mergers and acquisitions companies need to rely on English for effective communication. Even the European Commission with eleven official languages, recently switched to English as its official working language. Most of the companies like Nissan, Toyota circulate internal memos to colleagues in English regardless of where they are located.

Despite all efforts to standardise, the final language of communication is the language of the customer. It is his language and tastes the company has to adjust with. Hence not only English but the local language and culture of business have to be learnt. For example, a Japanese firm setting a branch in Saudi Arabia has to train his Japanese executives with English and Arabic languages too.

To avoid inconvenience:

— Learn the language of the country where the business is to be extended or where you are planning to settle.

— Use an intermediary or a translator to translate the business letters, specifically advertisements and user manuals.

— Avoid direct translation.

For effective intercultural communication a person has to identify the language barriers and modulate his oral and written skills according to his requirement. The best method is to improve his writing and speaking skills.

Adapt to the requirements and expectations of the reader. For instance, a Japanese begins with a formal goodwill enquiry, then may congratulate you with your success and finally reach to the main idea of writing the better. So if writing to a Japanese businessman, this method would be impressive. To be effective in writing one should be particular about: -

— Clarity of expression through concrete words.

— Consciousness of words likes climb instead of work up.

— Correctness in providing information.

— Courteous and polite in the conversational tone.

— Carefully planned and formatted from the reader's point of view.

It is easier to write in another language than to speak. However, one cannot avoid face-to-face conversation. To establish rapport one has to concentrate on verbal as well as non-verbal language. When an Englishman speaks to an ESL speaker he has to concentrate on:

— Clarity of his pronunciation by proper emphasis on contextual words.
— Feedback provided by the receiver through his body language.
— Rephrasing if necessary.
— Courtesy to ask "Am I going too fast?" but not "Is this too difficult for you?"
— Language used should not include idioms, fabulous and fantastic words.
— Use of foreign phrases for greetings.
— Listening to the speaker carefully and patiently.
— Adapting to the style of the speaker.

As teachers our aim is to help students overcome all the barriers of intercultural communication, may it be at the global level or the local level. Well-equipped labs with good spoken English CDs and high speed internet facilities can help us to refine the students to a large extent. But provision should be not only for English but also for other languages.

19

Role of English in Technical Education

Susama Panda

Technical field and language are both intricately intertwined and bring forth the latent personality in ourselves. The prerequisites of presentation of our national talents and technical skills are good communication skills and proper interaction. Presentation of national skills at an international conference demands the foundation to be very strong in English. The most interesting and felicitating aspect of English is that all technical institutions have made it a compulsory subject as the BPUT syllabus. This has made the students capable enough to express themselves comfortably at all interviews and campus recruitments in spite of their background schooling mediums.

The role of English is quite indispensable for its required interaction between institutions, between teaching staff and students, and among students themselves. English is a language that is accepted in latter day world in recognising every process in technical fields. Speak of astrophysics or nuclear physics or any kind of communication and what we need is merely English. All of our formats, formulations, communications as well as documentations are made in English.

Human beings are better recognised than other creatures for their effective medium of communication. We are to realise the importance of communication skills if we want to manifest our potentialities. How can we expect our exhibition and recognition of technological products in the arena of global trade and commerce effectively without proper presentation skills? Well, let me say these are the very essence of business aspect in technical field. And speaking in particular, communication ability is highlighted by one's gestures and postures that that we otherwise call as "Body Language". For instance, our eye expressions, hand movements and smiles while conversing with someone, especially with an interviewer or board member. There has to be an absolute wide awareness amongst students for building up an impressive body language. New, inexperienced but potential and innovative technocrats wouldn't be able to convince the executive board members and unless he or she has dynamic ambidextrous interpersonal skills.

Language on pen and paper has to be put forth in words that would be captivating as well as grammatically correct. Well, I am speaking of proper accent and phonetics. We, Indians, generally are backward in internationally acclaimed pronunciations. There should be a mass launch of accent improvement classes and seminars in all-technical institutions. There are some facets of personality development, which are sure to inculcate our strengths inherent in us manifold. I accentuate that communication and presentation skills as well as personality development and body language access, should be stressed to definite degrees in our institutions if we are to project forward with dogged confidence and optimism. I am absolutely sorry to say that all and sundry are not showing much inclination towards the procurement of efficiency in this medium of communication, because awareness is still lacking in us. And until and unless everyone is equally contributing towards the enhancement of a common medium, I insist, common medium, we cannot scud towards progress.

In today's changing global environment many organisations have voiced the need for new graduates of engineering programmes to have a stronger soft-skills emphasis. For example, employers need new graduates to be good communicators and to work in multidisciplinary teams of diverse cultural backgrounds and differing personality styles. Therefore, learning institutions that are able to align with industry demands to produce graduating engineers with the right kind of skills will reap substantial benefits. The integration of project management (PM) skills into the university engineering curriculum offers one solution for training and preparing students with the necessary transferable hard- and soft-skills from the classroom to the workplace. Unfortunately, essential non-technical skills are still lacking among engineering graduates because most engineering schools provide students with little practical experience and few applications competencies. These are the key features where the emphasis should be laid on:

- Improving communication and links between industry employers and educationists to create a clearer direction for student learning.
- Making the curriculum content more relevant to current and future needs of engineering organisations.
- Restructuring/redefining classroom pedagogy so that it incorporates essential skill-attributes.
- Encouraging students to obtain the needed skill-attributes through a structured and well-planned industrial internship programme, class projects/thesis, involvement with student and professional organisations and involvement in other campus organisations.
- Standardising and making essential soft-skills education compulsory in the engineering curriculum.

Changes in the engineering curriculum over the last decade have not been dynamic enough to keep pace with a rapidly-changing marketplace. Consequently, many graduates lack the essential skills on which to build new learning experiences. Thus curriculum changes are needed for engineering schools to stay relevant. Undoubtedly, this issue will present a big challenge for educators to design and implement effective learning strategies for soft-skills education into the engineering curriculum. A stronger emphasis on acquiring and practising soft-skills while at university is likely to better prepare students for the workplace. Not all students possess PM skills-attributes naturally, and hence students need help in acquiring soft-skills techniques to handle human-relationship issues that match employer expectations. Other ways of encouraging soft-skill development include co-op education, internships, mentoring, and by engaging students in practical real-world design problems and case studies. These should provide students with valuable opportunities for teamwork, problem solving, project planning/scheduling, people management, and communications.

The current employers' preference is to recruit graduates who have a solid foundation of both technical and non-technical skills because they are easy to train and become productive in a shorter time. Employers indicated they recruit fewer graduates from institutions whose courses do not respond to their skills requirements, or whose courses are seen as costly, inconvenient and not relevant to their immediate skill needs. Employers expect universities to carry out more research studies on industrial skill needs, and to keep their curricula relevant. Essentially, engineers possessing a high proficiency in both technical and PM soft skills competencies are better prepared to enter the working world. Many research findings support the trend toward seeing essential PM skills education as one method for addressing the soft-skills deficiency issues of new graduates. The principal skill gaps identified were attributed to skills such as interpersonal communication, project planning/scheduling, people management, problem-solving and team management. It is hoped that the results of this study will provide useful information to educators as input to review, study and reassess their present engineering curriculum.

Works Cited

Klukken, P.G., Parsons, J.R. & Columbus, P.J., The creative experience in Engineering practice: Implications for Engineering education, *Journal of Engineering Education*, 86(4), 133-138, 1997.

NSPE, Engineering education issues: Report on surveys of opinions of engineering deans and employers of Engineering graduates on the first professional degree *NSPE Publication No.* 3059, November, 1992.

Shtub, A., *Project Management: Engineering, Technology, and Implementation*, Engle Cliffs, N.J; Prentice, 1994.

20

Globalisation of Hinglish

—Deepanjali Mishra

"The world will speak Hinglish. Hinglish will soon become the most commonly spoken film of language globally, a leading British except of linguistics, David Crystal, predicted. If we take a statistical data, about more than one-third of Indians speak this language, which will increase in subsequent years. The main reason for this rise is extensive use of internet by the Indians. Internet speeds Hinglish like no other tool. Indian are among the forerunners of IT revolution. Therefore, Indian English or Hinglish will travel the globe and is likely to replace British and American form.

"I believe the mother tongue countries have had their day. It is now the turn of countries who's English is spoken as second language to take their lead," Crystal said in his lecture, "The Future of English" at the British Council one Saturday evening.

What is Hinglish? Well, Hinglish is an indigenous language of India. Hindi is the main language of the masses. More than half of India's population speak Hindi either as their mother tongue or they use it frequently at their work place, educational institute, etc. So when these people communicate in English, they frequently use Hindi words in between during the course of their conversation. This intermingled language, which is the mixture of Hindi and English is called Hinglish. But can this be considered as the birth of Hinglish? No, certainly not. Teenagers include it in conversation with their friends (read girlfriend). Therefore, indulges is a from and normal age. We can also say English speakers in India switch over to Hinglish when they feel they must do something desperately. Crystal argues that growth of population of Indian culture around the world including Bollywood movies, internet, mass media are responsible in a large way for the rise and spread of Indian English. This could also be considered as the birth of Hinglish.

Hindi is practised mostly by the people of northern India, Gujurat, and western India like Maharashtra, Rajasthan, Gujurat, etc. English is one of the mediums of education in many educational institutions. So the students who study English in their schools, mingle it with Hindi while communicating with their friends, family members, etc. Hinglish is getting popularity in some southern states also. People no longer have the feeling of hatred towards Hindi. They are interested to learn Hindi and they use some English words as a result of which they are very comfortable with Hinglish.

Reasons for Globalising Hinglish

One of the major reasons which are responsible for globalisation of Hinglish is Bollywood, which has given many movies and there are hundreds of movies which have made a mark in the united destined. There was a movie which came up with a title, Yeh Dil Mange More where Sahid Kapur played the lead role. Many of us might become much aware of the familiar song of Trimurti, "Duniya Re Duniya, Very Good Very Good, Duniyawale, Very Bad Very Bad, Uparwala, Very Good Very Good Nichewale Very Bad, Very Bad" which has contribution of Hindi and English words. Many bilingual films like Hyderabad Blues, pride and Prejudice are widely accepted by the Western countries. It is no longer consider as slang; rather the countries around the globe are generrously welcoming it.

Secondly, media is responsible in a large way for the rise and growth of Hinglish. If we turn on to any Indian television programme we hear words like, Hungry Kya? And What your bahana is? It has become an island of its own—a distinct hybrid of culture for people who aspire to make it nice without sacrificing the words of Hindi. It may soon claim some native speakers world wide. To emerge as the best and get maximum customers even the multinational companies resort to Hinglish. For example, one leading car manufacturer Ford sells Ikon car as the "josh machine" and Fusion as "Anything Karega" . The arch rivals Pepsi and Coca Cola also use Hinglish to compete with each other. If Pepsi uses the slogan 'Yeh Dil Mange More' Coke sells itself by using 'Life Ho To Aisi'. Two pizza companies, McDonald's and Domino Pizza which are continuously at war with each other, sell their products by using 'Hungry Kya'? and 'what your bahana is'? respectively. The practice of Hinglish is much commonly used by high profile media personalities, politicians, film stars, sports personlaties, to add glamour to their language. Most of the anchor persons make exensive use of Hinglish in television programmes, especially channel V and MTV. When the Star channels started channel V way back it was not as popular as it is now, when the producers decided to make it a Hinlish channel. Now we all can see the difference, Channel V has emerged as the most sought after channel in terms of viewership. This is the extract of the television interview of former Miss World and very popular movie actress, Aishwarya Rai where she uses Hinglish in a very casual way:

Q) Kya Aap Media Ke Upar Depend Karte Hai Ya Media Aapke Upar Depend Karta Hai?

Ans) Aishwarya: You know media Hamare Liye Saraswati Hai and Dono are made for each other.

The subcontimental tug of Hinglish is already being felt abroad. In Britan, the number one favourite meal is an Anglo-Indian invention called Chicken Tikka Masala.

Thirdly, internet is also responsible in a way for spreading Hinglish—random mixture of English and Hindi words used to form complete sentences, being categoried as another language. This actually originated in colleges, streets, telephones, internet, etc. If we want to send any virtual greeting in Hinglish, we just have to go to any e-greeting side like msn.com.or yahoo.com. These young boys and girls make extensive use of Hinglish and win while internet chatting or emailing. Recently Microsoft announced the company's decision to launch local versions of window and office Software in 14 Indian major languages. Hinglish is a welcome relief to those young talented people who are well equipped with all their skills but are not able to speak English. Hinglish can be used during interviews and in some cases it has fetched accolades too. They no longer need to feel embarrassed about it.

Therefore, we can say that Hinglish is a form of English that echoes a more polite and formal age. The previous longing to acquire a British or American accent has disappeared along with the sneers once prompted due to mispronunciation. Now, whenever an Indian word or an idiosyncrasy is being discussed the standard reaction is to laugh and say, "we are like that only". I conclude by saying that the words spoken by David Crystal is going to be a reality very soon.

21

Communicative Language Methods, Teaching Implication and Application in ELT

Smita Sinha

Effective communicative skills are the essential attributes of an impressive personality. Most of the existing language teaching methodologies emphasise only on the correct formation of grammatical sentences and interpretation of texts. They focus on developing the listening skill, speaking skills, reading skills and writing skills only. Very little attention has been given to the communicative skills as a tool for personality development and interpersonal skills. Communication does not mean only to speak and write. It has broad connotations. It means to articulate properly and to create an impact on the hearer.

Chomsky (1957) in *Syntactic Structure* stated that the current standard structural theories were not capable of accounting for the fundamental characteristic of language, the creativity and uniqueness of individual sentences. British applied linguists emphasized another fundamental dimension of language teaching at that time—the functional and communicative potential of language.

Communicative Method in ELT—Implication

Howatt (1984) wrote: "By the end of the sixties it was clear that the situational approach had run its own course. There was no future in continuing to pursue the chimera of predicting language on the basis of situational events. What was required was a closer study of the language itself and a return to the traditional concept that utterances carried meaning in themselves and expressed the meanings and intentions of the speakers and writers who created them" (pp. 280). Prior to this, popular language teaching methods such as direct method, grammar translation method, audio-visual and audio-lingual methods were very much in practice in most language teaching classrooms. Syllabuses in these classes were restricted to teaching of various literary works of noted poets and authors such as Shakespeare, Milton or Hardy, and the focus was primarily on the vocabulary building and understanding and analysing the texts. Very little attention was given to the practical use of these languages learnt in day-to-day use of communication, specially in official communications.

Wilkins (1972) proposed functional or communicative methods of teaching. Communicative definition of language serves as a base for developing communicative syllabuses for language teaching. Wilkin's contribution was an analysis of the communicative meanings that a language learner needs to understand and express. His revised and expanded book of 1972 called *Notional Syllabuses* (Wilkins (1976) had a significant impact on the development of communicative language teaching.

The scope of the communicative method is as follows:

— to make communicative competence the goal of language teaching.

— to develop procedures for teaching focus language skills that acknowledged the interdependence of language and communication.

Many linguists treat language teaching as an integration of grammatical and functional teaching. For Littlewood (1981), one of the most characteristic features of communicative language teaching is that it pays systematic attention to the functional as well as the structural aspect of language.

For many linguists it means using procedures where learners work in pairs or groups employing available language resources in problem-solving tasks. Howatt (1984) makes a distinction between a 'strong' and a 'weak' version of communicative language teaching. The 'weak' version which has become more or less standard practice in the last ten years, stresses the importance of providing learners with opportunities to use their English for communicative purposes and characteristically attempt to integrate such activities into a wider programme of language teaching. The 'strong' version of communicative teaching, on the other hand, advances the claim that language is acquired through communication. So it is not merely a question of activating an existing but inert knowledge of the language, of stimulating the development of the language system itself.

Finocchiaro and Brumfit (1983) present the distinctive feature of communicative approach in language teaching. They are:

— Meaning is permanent

— Dialogues, if used centre around communicative functions and not normally memorised.

— Contextualisation is a basic premise.

— Language learning is learning to communicate.

— Effective communication is sought.

— Drilling may occur but peripherally.

— Comprehensive pronunciation is sought

— Any advice, which helps tho learners, is accepted, varying according to their age, interest, etc.

— Attempts to communicate may be encouraged from the very beginning.

— Judicious use of native language is accepted, where feasible.

— Translation may be used, where students need or benefit from it.

— Reading and writing can start from the first day, if desired.

— The target linguistic system will be learned best through the process of struggling to communicate.

— Communicative competence is the desired goal (i.e., the ability to use the linguistic system effectively and appropriately).

— Linguistic variation is a central concept in material and methodology.

— Sequencing is determined by any consideration of content, function or meaning which maintains interest.

— Teaching helps learners in any way that motivates them to work with the language.

— Language is created by the individual, often through trial and error.

— Fluency and acceptable language is the primary goal. Accuracy is judged not in the abstract but in context.

— Students are expected to interact with other people, either through pair and group work or in their writings.

— Intrinsic motivation will spring from an interest in what is being communicated by the language.

The communicative competence theory contrasts Chomsky's theory of competence, i.e., the native speaker as the most competent speaker.

Canal (1983), Morrow (1977), Richards and Schmidt (1983) find the following characteristics in communication:

a) Is a form of social interaction, and is therefore normally acquired and used in social interaction.

b) Involves a high degree of unpredictability and creativity in form and message.

c) Takes place in discourse and socio-cultural contexts, which provide constraints on appropriate language use and also clues as to correct interpretations of utterances.

d) It is carried out under limiting psychological and other conditions such as memory constraints, fatigue and distractions.

e) Always has a purpose (for example to establish social relations, to pursuade or to promise).

f) Involves authentic, as opposed to text book, contrived language and

g) Is judged as successful or not on the basis of actual outcomes.

Communication is understood as the exchange and negotiation of information between at least two individuals through the use of verbal and non-verbal symbols, oral and written / visual modes and production and comprehension processes. Information is assumed to consist of conceptual, socio-cultural affective and other content.

Canale (1983) make a distinction between communicative competence and the actual communication. Communicative competence is understood as the underlying systems of knowledge and skill required for communication (e.g., knowledge of vocabulary and skills for a given language). Furthermore, a distinction was drawn between communicative competence and what is labelled as actual communication, the realisation of such knowledge and skill under limiting psychological and environmental conditions such as memory and perceptual constraints, fatigue, nervousness, distractions and interfering background noises. The term 'actual communicationer' is preferred since the earlier term 'performance' (or communicative performance) has been a source of confusion in applied linguistics since Chomsky's use of term 'performance' and 'competence' into modern linguistics. Regardless of the terminological shift, the view in Canale and Swain (1983) rephrased here is that communicative competence is an essential but is reflected only indirectly and sometimes imperfectly (e.g., in random and inadvertent slips of the tongue, mixing of registers) due to general limiting conditions such as those mentioned above.

Communicative competence refers to both knowledge and skill in using this knowledge when interacting in actual communication. Knowledge refers here to what one knows (consciously or unconsciously) about the language and about other aspects of communicative language use; skill refers to how well one can perform this knowledge in actual communication.

Torrell (1977) argues strongly that communication strategies are crucial at the beginning stages of second language learning. Two possible objections to actually teaching such strategies in the second language classroom are that they are universal and are picked up in mastering the first language. However, a general strategy such as a paraphrase is indeed universal and used in first language communication. Learners must be shown how such strategy can be implemented in the second language. The potential value of such strategies to the second language learner can perhaps be highlighted more if we think of the teacher of the second language as a learner of the first language. For example, consider a teacher of German as a second language, who speaks only German, to a group of Oriya learners. From the students' point of view, the teacher (speaking only German) can be viewed as a learner (of Oriya as a second language) who knows almost no Oriya and yet is trying to communicative effectively. To the extent that the teacher is understood by relying on communication strategies, then these strategies are crucial for communi-cation to take place at all.

The Study

Most of the teaching methodologies used in the secondary schools in Orissa are either grammar translation method (as in Oriya-medium schools), direct methods (as in English-medium ICSE or CBSE schools). In the Oriya-medium schools spoken elements are not at all given due consideration. Although in ICSE and CBSE schools, fluency is sought in speech, the syllabus covers more attention to analysis of texts. Letter writings do constitute the part of the examinations, but while teaching, less focus is given on the communicative methods of English language teaching. As a result, students from the Oriya-medium schools at college level and in professional life face great difficulties in communicative skills. Many English-medium students who are fluent in spoken English too at times are found fumbling at group discussions. In colleges too, the English subject paper concentrates on literature and its critical appreciation, grammar, essay and letter writing too. Since communicative skills are not given importance in the teaching process, many bright students fail to express themselves properly before an interview board for jobs.

In a pilot study done by me at Berhampur University in 2004 of the final year students, it is suggested that out of one hundred randomly picked up arts students 95 students could not speak for five minutes continuously and grammatically in English on any topic of their choice. The five students who could speak well were from the ICSE background. Among the science students 80 students could not speak grammatically, 15 students spoke grammatically, but the pronunciations were bad, only five students from ICSE background could speak in fluent English. All these students had first class or high second class marks in their part I PG examinations. What I observed is that as less of spoken elements constitute the teaching programme the students are not aware of the importance of communicative skills to prepare themselves for interviews and group discussions. Secondly, most of them are not polite in their speech.

Need for New Approach and Its Applications

Sinha (2005) found the need to use politeness in speech for effective communication. Expressions or sentences are not inherently polite or impolite. It is just the way they are used that make them politie or impolite. In the process of human communication, "the speaker is required to observe a certain extent of etiquette in his communicative behaviour as ordinarily by his community / societies. Part of the etiquette in the speech behaviour of every interaction lies in the maintenance of polite speech in one's discourse (Karunakaran, 1994: 133). Politeness is the basis for humility. It serves as a powerful weapon to settle unpleasant issues. It indicates good breeding and begets respect from others (Sinha, 2005).

While developing the communicative skills, the teacher, using the communicative method of language teaching, must look into the followings:

i. That the students are allowed to talk freely in the discourse.

ii. That the speech of the students are polite in all respects, because official communications are represented either through the forms of direct speech acts or through indirect acts as necessitated by the speech occasion. It also marks the power relationship between the participants. The language used in such communication speaks of the social distance, level of solidarity, level of dominance or affiliation between the speaker and the receiver. It also speaks of the attitude of the speakers and the relative status of a particular type of act, power, paradigm and level of intimacy.

iii. A lot of stress must be given to the correct vocabulary used in the discourse, because any wrong use of word can bring disaster to the situation.

iv. Emphasis on correct pronunciation, taking into account the diacritical features, must be sought. Suprasegmental features such as presupposition and focus can change the meaning of the utterances, for examples:

   a) John read a book.

   b) John read a book.

   Although both the sentences look same, they differ in meaning so far as the presupposition and focus are concerned. The first sentence presupposes that someone read a book and the focus is on John (and not Harry or Dick). The second sentence presupposes, John read something and focuses on book (and not on magazine). Although both the sentences are structured identical, they differ in meaning due to the way they are uttered (intonation pattern). Hence, care must be taken the way words and sentences are pronounced, as they have direct impact on the listeners.

v. Seeing the present day need of our students stress must be given on quickness. It is necessary to develop the skills in thinking quickly, and accurately and coherently, before uttering the sentences in proper discourses.

vi. A lot of mock interviews, group discussions and debates should constitute the part of language curriculum.

Conclusion

Since, in communicative language teaching methods, communicative competence is the desired goal, this method ranks above other methods of language teaching in present-day scenario. For implementing this the language teachers need proper orientations in an organised manner. As proper articulation is an essential feature of a good personality, the language teachers must look into the shortcomings of the individual learners and help them in developing proper communicative skills, taking the rules of etiquette and politeness in speech into consideration.

References

Canal, M., 'From communicative competence to language pedagogy, in Morrow, K.E. ed., *Techniques of Evaluation for a Notional Syllabus,* London: The Royal Society of Arts, 1977.

Chomsky, N., *Syntactic Structure*, The Hague: Moutan, 1957.

Finocchiaro, M. and C.J. Brumfet, *Functional–Notational Approach from Theory Practice* New York, 1983.

Howatt, A.P.R., *A History of English Language Teaching*. Oxford: OUP, 1984.

Karunakaran, K.V. Jaya and K. Kanchana, Politeness in Language use in the socio-cultural context of Tamils with reference to the administration Domain, In Koul, om. (ed.), *Language Development and Administration,* New Delhi, Creative Books, 1994.

Littlewood, W., *Communicative Language Teaching*, Cambridge, CUP, 1981.

Morrow, K.E. ed., *Techniques of Evaluation for a Notional Syllabus*, London: The Royal Society of Arts, 1977.

Richard, J.C. and R.W. Schmidt, *Language and Communication* (eds.) New York: Longman, 1983.

Sinha, S., Workplace harassment on women and role of politeness in official language use-A Study, in Gupta and Sinha (eds.), *Empowerment of Women: Language and Other Facets.* Jaipur: Mangaldeep Publications, 2005.

Terrell, T.D., 'A natural approach to second language acquisition and learning', *The Modern Language Journal*, 61/7, 325-37, 1977.

Wilkins, D.A., *Linguistics in Language Teaching. London*: Edward Arnold, 1976, *National Syllabus*, Oxford: OUP, 1972.

22

How to Teach English: The Process of Teaching English

Subash Chandra Pati

The process of teaching English in India poses a major problem—whether to teach it as a language or a literature. Unless a student has a special interest he seems to be reluctant to read English as a literature. A majority of students prefer to read it as a language and an effective means of self-expression. A teacher cannot ignore this aspect while teaching English. Quite naturally, we come to the conclusion that we should have to devise effective ways of teaching English, which will increase the language proficiency of students both in writing and in speaking. The achievement of this goal necessitates the active involvement of the student in the teaching process. The traditional lecture method must be substituted by the two-way teaching learning method. In this process, the teacher and the students should act as a harmonious unit, both playing their role effectively.

Language study has special significance in technical education. Expressing in technical field, one should avoid vagueness and unnecessary elaboration. So, we can conclude that expression in this field should have precision and clarity. To be successful in this respect a student should possess adequate selective vocabulary and should learn how to utilise this vocabulary to serve his purpose. To develop this skill the teacher should be a willing giver of language skill whereas the student should be a keen and willing receiver. The class room should be a co-operative endeavour among the Teacher, a pariticular learner and the rest of the learners in the classrooms. The concept of the students as passive listeners and a teacher as an unobstructed speaker is to be done away with. The teacher will give the clues. Some selective reference materials and relevant dictionary will aid the process of development of a student's skill. Mutual interaction between the teacher and the learner and among the learners will help the learner adequately.

Besides the above method, comprehension work and paragraph writing on a particular topic, events and problems will enhance the language skill of a technical student. Comprehension work will increase his power to understand whereas, paragraph writing will develop his concept and imaginative power. He will learn how to approach a thing or idea and how to express it before others.

The language learning process of technical student should have a definite orientation. Besides a command over general vocabulary, he should be proficient in the vocabulary relevant to his subject and work. These are the primary equipments. Added with a sound imagination, intelligence and clarity of thought these equipment's will shape a satisfactory communicative skill.

In the field of technology, clarity of expression is very significant. Here ideas should not be expressed in ambiguous and complex terms as is done in philosophy, and at times in Literature. Such tendency will mar the communication process in the technical field. So the basic necessity is to create an orientation in the mind of such students. Bseides Comprehension work and the paragraph writing, some model writings should be presented to the students who will serve as silent teachers. Thus it becomes clear that effective and practical classroom teaching and individual endeavour are equally important in the process of language learning.

A major obstacle was clearly the grading system. You can tell students anything you want about "taking responsibility" and "thinking for yourself". The grading system you employ—a middle finger extended before them—is always more eloquent still. It has nothing to do with literature, it has nothing to do with composition; that it appears so is only a measure of the way it has reshaped these subjects in its own image. For many of our students (and for some of us perhaps), grading consitutes a sort of Marxian base, a bedrock reality, compared to which the actual subject matter itself seems secondary and less real. The grading system tends to drive a class. What it does to students is in great part what "The Student as Nigger" is all about.

In an admirable earlier essay, "The Peaceable Classroom", O'Reilly suggests that "as teachers in the humanities, the most important thing we are able to do is encourage our students in their expoloration of the inner life" (110). But when we grade a person C+ on his inner life, "encourage" takes on a more sinister meaning. I think of what Voltaire tells us, " pour encourager les autres."

We complain about students' intellectual passivity, or even torpor. We mock their obsession with "what's going to be on the final." But that's like complaining about the laziness of slaves. Who do we think created these monsters? Is it really true that things have changed, that, as O'Reilly maintains, our students "have been dosed with progressive education since pre-school"? I am not sure what she means by "progressive" or what may be happening in St. Paul, but in San Diego, where I have three children in the public school system and one in the university, there has been little structrual change. I have seen good teaching occasionally, esecially at the pre-schools that still foster "slave mentality" which I described in 1967 and which O'Reilly says she continues to encounter. When are we teachers going to understand that much of what we deplore in students is actually functional, that they are responding with at least some intelligence, not to what we say, but to what we do ?

This arrangement, however, is vulnerable to attack from two directions. From one side, someone could say, "Look, you're still pushing students around. You're still keeping them in bondage; they're just happier about it."

But then there's the argument from the other side. "Exactly !" some might say. taining the productivity and the standard that keep civilisation alive." This critic could point out that, though my approach to grading may well guarantee that anyone who gets through the course has met the core requirements, it doesn't adequately differentiate between A, B, and C students, since a very hard-working student might pick up an A without doing what might generally be regarded as A-level work. That's exactly right, and I could care less. As a matter of fact, I would be delighted to see that person working so hard.

But students, I would argue, don't exist, unless we create them. How ironic that we who concern ourselves with language and who, in our sophistication, distance ourselves from so many categories, so many social constructs, should cling so tightly to this one. But of course we do; it entitles us—literally. We have been willing to deconstruct everying in sight except our own august pondium. A "student" is not merely someone who happens to be, say, learning Italian. He is a member of a group into which we shamelessly project our own corporate and individual mythologies and in relation to which we construct our own identity as teachers. Among us, the brutal overseer and the idealising social worker are inhabiting the same metaphysic. Given the right circumstances one can convert it to the other.

As teachers, we tend to grab power, to exercise it far beyond what is necessary; we get hung up on it, we mususe it. Too often we keep for ourselves the power that we should be helping others to develop (the way literature typically has been taught provides an excellent example of this). And all of this power-tripping, unfortunately, fits into larger patterns of social oppression.

If our ambitions for teaching are modest, perhaps we can hope to exclude this messy and pronblematic mode and run things on a clear-cut business basis. Certainly, I am all for demystifying teaching and for deflating th romanticised image that people can sometimes form of a teacher. But if teaching addresses and affects what matters most in human life, if it insists on overflowing the borders that are laid out for it, if it exists by virtue of the possiblility of transformation, then though we may well choose to play down love, to let it work in slilence—I am more than comfortable doing that—we shouldn't deceive ourselves about it.

We have to discuss the stages of learning which is absolutely essential in the spoken field for a technocrat. In the field of technology method of learning, method of self study and the benefit of learning are necessary. These stages are shown in process given below:.

Stages:

1. General Conversation — Fromal- Informal—Telephonic
2. Answering interview—Frequently asked questions
3. Public Speaking - Seminar - Meeting — Anchoring — Discussion.

In the method of listening to pronounciation, intonation and vocabulary are needed. Pronounciation deals with proper accented descent. We clearly intimate our emotion with proper emphasis, and our narration should be clear. In the same way we shoued absorb strong vocabularies, phonetic device and thorough knowledge for reading. Our voice should be clear and bold. In the field of self-study reading english journal and books, listening to news on radio and television and Group discussion supports a lot for improvement. Taking structure into account, gramatical correctness is above all important in the field of communication.

We come accross different grades of speakers of English. They are limited users, intermittent users, rare users, moderate users, expert users, good users and competent users. In learning English there are different areas. Those telephone, debate assignments, interviews, taking initiative in conversation speaking in informal situation, introducing a person to another person, a discussion in formal situation on a specific topic, speaking to a celebrity, simple conversation in day-to-life, a business talk, delivering lecture and so on.

The problem areas we face in communication mostly are on breathing, understanding, pausing, clarity, voice, shyness, pronounciation, vocabulary, structure, grammar accuracy, listening, etc. We also see differences type of speakers. They are slow talkers, nasal talkers, shriekers, lazylips, foghorn, husky and so on. At times speech blemishes occurs. These blemishes are apolegetic beginning, jargon, meaningless words and phrases, copycat, lack of audience contact, repitition, lack of grace and enthusiasm, 'er' and 'er' habits.

To explain more elaborately, the learning areas in the communication ground are the ability to ask questions, intimation, the ability to take inititative, proper pronounciation, general fluency, structural accuracy, communicate effectively, proper vocabulary skill, ability to answer with appropriate vocabulary and structure.

We need the folllowing remedies to rectify our spoken English. We need to enjoy public gathering, meeting and party. We should concentrate on our own business. We must have perfect endurance to servive in an English-speaking environment with self-respect. We should be involved in the interview profession.

In order to upgrade our speaking skills it is a continuous process of improvement without any full stop. We should get practise in meeting people, speaking different languages, recording, discussing reading magazines and journals, listening to radio and watching television and learning new words.

Vivid corrections are made in different scriptures for our personal development. In the *Bhagavad Gita*, Chapter 13 Shlokas 7 -11-Lord Krishna admonished Arjuna in the battle-field of Kurukshetra in a clear manner. Human being is a social being and most of the problems arise before him. He should not be obstructed. The obstruction can only occure by our lacuna in personality which make us survive in the global, developing and marvellous world. So, we should find the basic solution to our hindrance. We should not be egocentric, insincere, lifeless, argumentative, condescending, exaggerative, dogmatic, mumbling, but aim to be the life of a party. Such correction with will provide us-self-confidence, knowledge, initiativeness and preparedness for a quick driving force to enter into a better and greater state of life.

We should accept proper responsbility, friendliness, cheerfullness, tactfulness with a promotive sense. Other than these, there should be involvement, flexibility, courageousness, courteousness unlocking our real personality getting interested, without stopping learning, and sound understanding of the world. A techno is expected to be practise strong enough in these levels to florish in the world.

The experiments and findings in the field of technology require clear explication. In view of this necessity, language study constitutes an essential part of technical education. Without effective, appropriate and imaginative language the acievements of technology cannot be brought outside the laboratories. When we tell appropriate we do not mean a dull and monotonous expression. Naturally, a student of technology finds it difficult to be appropriate and imaginative at the same time. Hence, language study is a very important aspect in technical education.

23

Passage to Global Citizenship— The Role of English

Gouri Shankar Patnaik

Introductory

In a world where every aspect of life is increasingly dependent upon scientific and technological progress, promoting literacy and education in multiple strata through English is indispensable for all nations, not only to achieve sustainable development but also to create a developed literate mass in the interests of ensuring true democracy.

English has become a world language, spoken by at least 750 million people. It is more widely spoken and written than any other language, even Latin, has ever been. It can, indeed, be said to be the first truly global language. To have an introspect into the history, many languages have donned the role as an international tool for communication, but for a short span. During the history of mankind, there have been several more or less universal languages or lingua francas, such as Latin (and Greek) in the Roman empire, mediaeval Latin in Western Europe, later French and English.

At the dawn of civilisation in the ancient Middle East, Egyptian rose to pre-eminence among nations; but by the end of the Middle Ages it was extinct. In the Hellenistic period, Greek was spoken all the way from Athens to the banks of the Amu Darya in Central Asia; now it is confined to the southern extremity of the Balkan peninsula. Latin once reigned supreme over the European territory south of the Danube and west of the Rhine, not to mention North Africa; it even survived the fall of Rome by well over a millennium. Today Latin is no longer used for communication (except in the Vatican), and appears to be rapidly disappearing from school curricula.

Universality is of course relative; it means universality in the "known world" or "civilised world", or just in a large empire. No language has been really universal (global), but the current position of English comes the closest. A natural, national language used outside its national boundaries by other peoples can serve as an international language. Latin, for instance, was a universal language in Europe during the Middle Ages and the Renaissance. French was once known as the universal language of diplomacy, and English today is often said to fill such a role in world commerce. The English language has grown up in contact with many others making it a hybrid language, which can rapidly evolve to meet new cultural and communicative needs.

Spoken by about 470 million people throughout the world, English is the official language of about 45 nations. It is the mother tongue of about 60 million persons in the British Isles, from where it spread to many other parts of the world owing to British exploring, colonising, and empire-building from the seventeenth through nineteenth centuries. It is now also the first language of an additional 228 million people in the United States; 16.5 million in Canada; 17 million in Australia; 3 million in New Zealand and a number of Pacific islands; and approximately 15 million others in different parts of the Western Hemisphere, Africa, and Asia. As a result of such expansion, English is the most widely scattered of the great speech communities. It is also the most commonly used auxiliary language in the world. The United Nations uses English not only as one of its official languages but also as one of its two working languages.

English can be easily staged as an international language, because it is a language used by people of different linguistic backgrounds to facilitate communication among them and to reduce the misunderstandings and antagonisms caused by language differences. An international language is usually intended not to supplant existing mother tongues but to play a secondary or auxiliary role as it furthers international communication. And, English rightly chips in the role of an international language. But, for the first time in history, due to the high-end developments and technological progress, it is possible to speculate about the emergence of a global language in English.

Historical Perspective

Britain's colonial expansion established the pre-conditions for the global use of English, taking the language from its island birthplace to settlements around the world. As regards to the English language, it would have remained as a national language of the English, had it not happened so that the English first conquered the rest of the British Isles, then many other parts of the world. Later, some English colonies in a relatively small part of America rebelled, formed the United States of America, and expanded a lot. They formed a federal state where a variant of the English language was one of the few really uniting factors.

The story of English in the twentieth century has been closely linked to the rise of the US as a superpower, which has spread the English language alongside its economic, technological, and cultural influence. In the same period, the international importance of other European languages, especially French, has declined. Today's English is the continuation of the language of the fifth-century Germanic invaders of Britain. No records exist of pre-invasion forms of the language. The language most closely related to English is the West Germanic language Frisian.

The history of English is an aspect of the history of the English people and their development. Thus in the ninth century the standard English was the dialect of dominant Wessex. The Norman Conquest (11th century) brought in foreign rulers, whose native language was Norman French; and English was eclipsed by French as the official language. When English became again (14th century) the language of the upper class, the capital was London, and the new standard (continued in Modern Standard English) was a London dialect. The most important reason for the success of English is naturally the historical role of England as a colonial power.

It is convenient to divide English into periods—Old English (or Anglo-Saxon; to century 1150), Middle English (to century 1500), and Modern English; this division implies no discontinuity, for even the hegemony of French affected only a small percentage of the population. The English-speaking areas have expanded at all periods. Before the Normans the language was spoken in England and Scotland, but not in Cornwall, Wales, or, at first, in Strathclyde. English has not completely ousted the Celtic languages from the British Isles, but it has spread vastly overseas.

English came to be the language of the legal system, higher education, administrative network, science and technology, trade and commerce—either because the indigenous languages were not equipped for these roles and English provided for a convenient vocabulary, or because the use of English was considered prestigious and powerful. English became gradually a major tool for acquiring knowledge. It has come to represent modernisation and development, and, as a link language, it has acquired international roles over the years. It is a matter of statistical fact that English is the most important world language. It is the language of modernity, of the twenty-first century—the language of the most advanced technologies, of air traffic, computing, telecommunications, the language of world politics, diplomacy and international finance.

Some other reasons for the dominance of English around the world are its propensity for acquiring new identities, its power of assimilation, its manifestation in a range of lects, and its provision of a flexible medium for literary and other types of creativity across languages and cultures. The geopolitical dominance of English is henceforth well ensured and is backed by a relatively homogeneous international usage in writing, but often influenced in the spoken language by the linguistic, cultural, and social diversity of the speakers, and even different from the best accepted styles of the big Anglophone countries. International relations of all kinds— media, music, business documents—contribute to its spreading.

MOVING FURTHER

Moving in the direction of English as an international language, we must rethink several assumptions. As an incredibly globally spread language, English should no longer be considered as a property of its native speakers. It has already grown into a world property. With no attempt to de-emphasize the national practice of English for English-speaking countries, the international function of English is thought to be a different aspect, which deserves particular attention. The existence of different varieties for English warns us against the danger of limiting the scope of practice and learning to certain limited varieties. Accordingly students are suggested that they should get familiar with different varieties, native and non-native. Our curriculum for teaching English should, thus, be improved with the inclusion of varieties of English spoken by different native or non-native speakers. This measure will help students broaden their appreciation and knowledge of the language they use and get prepared for any variety not yet known to thom.

As far as the culture is concerned, due to the diversity among native speakers on the one hand, and the heterogeneous population of non-native speakers on the other, the culture of native speakers can no longer be imposed. In contrast to the idea of language hegemony or linguistic chauvinism, non-native speakers of English may use it to express, react or even propagate their ideas to affect a relatively larger part of the world, including native speakers. The increasing trend of globalisation may indirectly make us take immediate measures to live up to the demands of the oncoming era, one of whose basic demands is the ability and readiness to communicate and understand via an international language. Thus it seems urgent that individuals in all parts of the world be adequately equipped with this effective tool as soon and as much as possible.

English is the language most frequently used in international trade, diplomacy and tourism and that it is studied by more people than any other language. Reports reveal that non-native speakers of English comprise more than two-thirds of its potential speakers. This seems to be an appropriate edge to argue that English, in international settings, does not belong to any one group of people. In fact, people from different nations all around the world may adopt this key for a variety of reasons. Under these conditions, for overcoming misunderstandings a process of mutual adjustment amongst interactors may automatically be activated.

English, as an international language is intercultural. The use of English and any other language is always culture bound, but the language itself is not bound to any specific culture or political system. In English as Foreign Language specific varieties of English and specific cultures can be dealt with. This may not be considered valid for English as International Language (EIL). It is clear that in teaching of EIL the goal cannot be knowledge of details of a given variety or culture or even numbers of these. The ways of speaking and the patterns of discourse are different across cultures. Americans may speak English natively yet may not be properly understood by a Briton. A native English-speaking Australian may have similar problems with an American or an Indian. In fact, English is an exceptional natural language able to obtain international appreciation.

English as International Language refers to functions of English not to the given form of the language. Thus it is concerned with the use of English by people of different nations and different cultures in order to communicate with one another. It is conceptually different from Basic English. It differs from English for Special Purposes (ESP) as well in the sense that it is not limited to any specific domain or field. As there are many varieties of English, EIL is an intervarietal way of communication. From the EIL perspective no speaker is realised as extreme. The listener can be any speaker of English, native or non-native. In addition, experience points out the learners' need to prepare for understanding intervarietal spoken English in face-to-face interactions.

As far as spoken English is concerned, Received Pronunciation (RP) may no longer be considered the ultimate model. The acquisition of native-like accent is no longer the ultimate objective of the majority of the learners. This assumption has also been asserted by many researchers since language pedagogy is taking a more positive view than it did in the past of the existence of varieties of language, dialects and sociolects within a speech community.

As a lingua franca of the past century and the new millennium, English is one of the most important means for acquiring access to the world's intellectual and technical resources. Though it may be due to vestige of British colonism or the sign of the American cultural imperialism, English is now seen less as a symbol of imperialism and more as a viable candidate for the world's most important international language. At this point in the world's history, English is the pre-eminent language of wider communication. It is rightly used as a library language, as the medium of science, technology and international trade, and as a contact language between nations and parts of nations. And, this is the only force to bring world together.

Works Cited

Crystal, David, *The English Language*, London: Penguin Books, Ltd, 1983.

Kachru, Braj B., The Indianisation of English, *The English Language in India,* Oxford: OUP, 1983.

Smith, L. E. & Rafiqzad, English for cross-cultural communication: the question of intelligibility, In L.Smith 1983, *Readings in English as an international language,* Pergamon Press, 1979.

Prodromou, L., "English as Cultural Action", *ELT Journal*, 42/2, 1988,

24

Variations in English Language, Pronunciation and Mother-tongue Influence

R.C.Thakur

We have largely ignored the fact that every language will have more than one variety, especially in the way in which it is spoken. Yet this variation in speech is an important and well recognised aspect of our daily lives as language-users in different regional and social communities. Here, we shall consider the type of variation which has been investigated via a form of linguistic geography, concentrating on regional varieties, and then we shall consider the factors involved in social variation in language use.

Standard language

When we described the sounds, words and sentences of English, we were, in fact, concentrating on the features of only one variety, usually labelled Standard English. This is the variety which forms the basis of printed English in newspapers and books, which is used in mass media and which is taught in schools. It is the variety we normally try to teach those who want to learn English as a second language. It is clearly associated with education and broadcasting in public contexts and is more easily described in terms of written language, i.e. vocabulary, spelling, grammar, than the spoken language.

If we are thinking of that general variety used in public broadcasting in the United States, we can refer more specially to Standard American English or in Britain, to Standard British English. There is no reason why other national varieties such as Standard Australian English, Standard Canadian English and Standard Indian English should not be recognised also.

Accent and Dialect

Whether or not you think you speak a standard variety of English, you will certainly speak with an accent. It is a myth that some speakers have accents while others do not. Some speakers may have distinct or easily recognised types of accent while others do not, but every language speaks with an accent. The term accent, when used technically, is restricted to the description of aspects of pronunciation which identify where an individual speaker is from, regionally or socially. It is to be distinguished from the term dialect which describes features of grammar and vocabulary, as well as aspects of pronunciation. For example, the sentence "You don't know what you're talking about" will generally look the same whether spoken with an American or a Scottish accent. Both speakers will be using Standard English forms, but have different pronunciations. There are, of course, differences in pronunciation, but there are also examples of different vocabulary and a different grammatical form.

While differences in vocabulary are often easily recognised, dialect variations in the meaning of grammatical constructions are less frequently documented.

Despite occasional difficulties, there is a general impression of mutual intelligibility among many speakers of different dialects, or varieties, of English. The point to remember is that, from a linguistic point of view, no one variety is better than another. They are simply different. From a social point of view, however, some varieties do become more prestigious. In fact, the variety which develops as the Standard Language has usually been one socially prestigious dialect, originally connected with a political or cultural centre (i.e. London for British English, and Parish for French). Yet, there always continue to be other varieties of language, spoken in different regions.

Regional Dialects

The existence of different regional dialects is widely recognised and often the source of some humour for those living in different regions. Thus, in the United States, someone from Brooklyn may joke about the Southerner's definition of "sex" by telling you that sex is fo'less than tin, in his best imitation of someone from the Southern States. The Southerner can, in return, wonder what a tree guy is in Brooklyn, since he has heard Brooklyn speakers refer to doze tree guy.

Some regional dialects clearly have stereotyped pronunciations associated with them. Those involved in the serious investigation of regional dialects are fairly uninterested in such stereotypes, however, and have devoted a lot of research to the identification of consistent features of speech found in one geographical area rather than another. After all, it is important to know if the person whose speech you are tape recording really is a typical representative of the region's dialect and the representative might be older, rural, male or female. Such speakers were selected because it was believed that they were less likely to have influences from outside the region in their speech.

Isoglosses and Dialect Boundaries

Let us take a look at some examples of regional variation found in one survey, that which resulted in the Linguistic Atlas of the Upper Midwest of the United States. One of the aims of such a survey is to find a number of significant differences in the speech of those living in different areas and to be able to chart where the boundaries are, in dialect terms, between those areas. If it is found, for example, that the vast majority of informants in one area say that they take their groceries home in a paper bag while the majority in another area say they use a paper sack, then it is usually possible to draw a line across a map separating the two areas. This line is called an Isogloss and represents a boundary between the areas with regard to that one particular linguistic item. If a very similar distribution is found for another two items, such as a preference for pail to the north and for bucket to the south, then another isogloss, probably overlapping, can be drawn in. When a number of isoglosses come together in this way, a more solid line, indicating a dialect boundary, can be drawn.

So, if an American English speaker pronounces the word greasy as (grizi) and takes groceries home in a paper sack, then he is not likely to have grown up and lived most of his life in Minnesota. It is worthnoting that the characteristic forms are used by everyone living in that region. They are used by a significantly large percentage of the people in a particular region.

The Dialect Continuum

The drawing of isoglosses and dialect boundaries is quite useful in establishing a broad of regional dialects, but it tends to obscure the fact that, at most dialect boundary areas, one variety merges into another. Keeping this in mind, we can view regional variation as existing along a continuum, and not as having sharp breaks from one region to the next. A very similar type of cotinuum can occur with related languages existing on either side of a political border. For this reason, people on or near the bordering areas of two nations of different languages have their dialects less clearly differentiated.

Speakers who move back and forth across this border, using different varieties with some ease, may be described as bidialectal (i.e., speaking two dialects). Most of us grow up with some form of bidialectalism, speaking one dialect in the street and having to learn another dialect in the school. However, if we want to talk about people knowing two distinct languages, we have to describe them as being bilingual.

BILINGUALISM

In many countries, regional variation is not simply a matter of two dialects of a single language, but a matter of two quite distinct and different languages. Canada, for example, is an officially bilingual country, with both French and English as official languages. This recognition of the linguistic rights of the country's French speakers largely in Quebec, did not come about without a lot of political upheaval. For most of its history, Canada was essentially an English-speaking country, with a French-speaking minority group. In such a situation, bilingualism, at the individual level, tends to be a feature of the minority group. In this form of bilingualism, a member of a minority group grows up in one linguistic community, primarily speaking one language, such as Welsh in Wales, Gaelic in Scotland or Spanish in the United States, but learn another language, such as English, in order to take part in the larger, dominant, linguistic community.

Indeed, many members of linguistic minorities can live out their entire lives without ever seeing their native language appear in the public domain. Sometimes political activism can change that. It was only after English notices and signs were frequently defaced or replaced by scribbled Welsh-language versions that bilingual (English-Welsh) signs came into widespread use in Wales.

SOCIAL FACTORS

Socio-linguistics deals with the interrelationships between language and society. It has strong connections to anthropology, through the investigation of language and culture, and to sociology, through the crucial role that language plays in the organisation of social groups and institutions.

In modern studies of language variation a great deal of care is taken to document, usually via questionnaires, certain details of the social backgrounds of speakers.

Two obvious factors in the investigation of social dialect are social class and education. In some dialect surveys, it has been found that, among those leaving the educational system at an early age, there is a greater tendency to use forms which are relatively infrequent in the speech of those who go into college. It seems that a person who spends a long time going through college or university will tend to have spoken language features which derived from a lot of time spent working with the written language. That is why, sometimes, it is said that some professor "Talks like a book". It is possibly a recognition of an extreme form of this influence.

The social classes also sound different. According to a famous study by Labov in 1972 in New York, variation in pronunciation is also influenced by the occupational conditions and the economic status of the speakers. As a result, it was concluded "The higher the economic status the more the sounds, and the lower the socio-economic status, the fewer the sounds produced." So, the difference in a single consonant could mark higher versus lower social class.

Age and Gender

Even within groups of the same social class, other differences can be found such as the age or gender of speakers. Variations according to age is most noticeable across the grandparent-grandchild timespan.

Female speakers tend to use more prestigious forms than male speakers with the same general social background. Quite different pronunciations of certain words in male and female speech have been documented in some North American Indian languages such as Gross Ventre and Koasati. Indeed, when Europeans first encountered the different vocabularies of male and female speech among the Carib Indians, they reported that the different sexes used different languages. There are also differences in the talk of males and females. Women generally prefer to discuss their personal feelings more than men. There is a pattern documented in American English social contexts of women cooperating and seeking connection via language, whereas men are more competitive and concerned with power via language.

Language and Culture

Many of the factors which give rise to linguistic variation are sometimes discussed in terms of cultural differences. It is not unusual to find linguistic features quoted as identifiable aspects of working class culture or African–American culture. This view has been influenced by the work of anthropologists who tend to treat language as one element among others, such as beliefs, within the definitions of culture as socially acquired knowledge. Given the process of cultural transmission by which languages are acquired, it makes a lot of sense to emphasize the fact that linguistic variation is tied very much to the existence of different cultures.

Idiolect

Of course, the aspects of all these elements of social and regional dialect variation are combined, in one form or another, in the speech of each individual. The term idiolect is used for the personal dialect of each individual speaker of a language. Other factors, such as voice, quality and physical state also contribute to the identifying features in an individual's speech.

In the Backdrop

English is spoken as a first language and as second language by a large number of people in many countries of the world. The variety of English spoken in the United Kingdom is different from the one spoken in America and other countries. The English spoken in England is quite different from the English spoken in Scotland or Ireland because there are a number of regional dialects of English in England itself. This is also true in case of the languages spoken in South Asian countries. In India, too, the pronunciation of English differs from one state to another state.

Colonial Impact

The countries which experienced the colonial rule of the British generally follow the dialect known as the educated southern British English (popularly known as received pronunciation—R.P, i.e., widely accepted variety. This kind of English is spoken by a very small percentage of people in the UK and other countries although it is recognised as a standard form of English in international communication. Recently, American English has also influenced the speakers of South Asian countries through tourism, radio, television and other media of mass communication. As a result, a mixture of South Asian, British and American varieties of English has come into existence and become common. However, it is not necessary that South Asian speakers should follow the R.P. (Received Pronunciation). We must cultivate the practice of distinguishing between sounds and phonetic variations (variations in speech features). Hence, more emphasis should be given to the fact that communication should be clear, effective and intelligible. On the other hand, students may be advised to acquire adequate command over both spoken and written English till the time of finishing their educational level.

Gender-based Variation

Latest researches based on dialect surveys tell that female speakers tend to use more prestigious forms than male speakers with the same general social background. I DONE IT and HE DIDN'T are more often found in the speech of males whereas I DID IT, HE ISN'T in the speech of females.

There are some differences in the talk of males and females in contemporary English also. Women generally discuss their personal experiences, feeling connected with themselves. And on the other side, men tend to prefer non-personal topics like sports and news. So, the tone also seems to change positively depending upon the sensitivity of topics.

Influence of Mother Tongue on English Pronunciation

Reasons

1. Each language has its own sound system and organisation of structure.

2. After learning a language, the learner reproduces it according to what he hears around the particular language community.
3. During the course of learning a language, the learner forms some certain habits of pronunciation.
4. Native language interference—while learning his mother tongue the learner has to perform practices of pronunciation since early childhood and based on traditional tone of language followed by a society.

Some Forms of Native Language Interference

1. A non-native learner of English faces problems in pronouncing certain vowel and consonant sounds of English accurately because those sounds do not occur in the mother tongue. In English, the central ?, the back rounded vowel É, and the consonants f,v,?,O,t,f,d? are particularly difficult. The English phonemes f,v are heard and pronounced by many speakers as ph, bh.
2. The consonant clusters in English such as street, school, sports are often difficult for Hindi speakers. So, they normally insert a vowel at the beginning of the word to break up the clusters. For example, the clusters - str- , sk-, and sp- are pronounced as is-tr, is-k-, and is-p-.
3. Many languages in South Asian countries have the two phonemes W and Y, but in practice we fail to make distinction required in English. The words wool and wood tend to be pronounced without the w sound, and the words yellow and yesterday without the y sound.
4. We feel it difficult to distinguish between the strong stressed and the weak unaccented syllables in English. The main cause behind this is that our native languages do not have a weakening of the unstressed syllables and stress as a speech feature is weaker than in English. So we people tend to stress the weak syllables and the accented syllables with equal force. Consequently, the rhythm of our spoken sound becomes very unnatural and artificial.

5. Many languages in north India and Nepal have Devanagari script where writing is quite close to the phonetic contrast in sounds. This is the reason that we tend to pronounce English words as they are spelt, thus ignoring the considerable difference between spelling and pronunciation.
6. The English voiceless plosives p, t, k are normally aspirated in stressed initial positions. This aspiration sounds so weak to the South Asian speakers that they do not regard these sounds as equivalent to their own aspirated plosives ph, th, kh and we tend to use unaspirated plosives p, t, k while speaking English.

Some examples of Differences between British R.P. and South Asian Pronunciation

Word	British R.P.	South Asian P
1. Between ?u and É:		
Coat	k?ut	ko:t
Course	kÉ:s	ko:rs
2. Between ^ ? and ?:		
Bud	b^d	b?d
Bird	b?:d	b?rd
3. F, V(R P) Replaced by ph bh		
Fine	Fain	Phain
Very	Veri	Bheri
4. Existence of r in all positions		
Heard	h?:d	h?rd
Error	er?	er?e
5. Dropping of W and J in South Asian English		
Wool	Wul	Ul
Yes	Jes	Es

Despite continuous efforts by phoneticians and linguists much has not been gained in this regard, because, the shape and size of the organs of speech also differ in different regions depending upon geographical conditions. On the other hand, English language has attained global status which is the need of the present growing computerised industrialisation and technological advancement. So this pronunciation factor stands sheltered to the convenience of the people of the concerned area. However, some suggestions deserve to be mentioned.

Suggestions

1. Dictionaries, containing references to pronunciation, may be consulted by students or readers. This will help them find out correct distribution of English vowels and consonant.
2. The vowels in unaccented syllables should be weakened. If we tend to speak English with only strong forms, this will sound unnatural. The words such as and, as, than, that, was, to, for, from, them, etc., are normally weakened.
3. English vowels and diphthongs should be clearly distinguished to show contrasts and variations existing within the language.
4. The variations in vowel qualities in extended word formations and the loss of vowels (elision) in connected speech need to be practised

   Examples : Pronounce à Pronunciation

   Origin à Original
5. Clear distinction should be maintained in S and ? i.e. sip and sheep and between Z and ? i.e. - Zip - Jeep.
6. The voiceless stops p, t, k should be aspirated in stressed initial position.
7. The phoneme r should be spoken or dropped for the convenience in the pronunciation.
8. Systematic practice of vowel and consonant sound symbol may be done to achieve possible success.
9. The most important point to note here is that clarity of pronunciation is essential for any speaker to convey the accurate message to the listener to whom it is intended.

25

Administrative Communication

Shalini

The word communication is the noun form of the word communicate which comes from the word "communicare", that means to impart, to give or to make common we know what ever is common is shared by all. Communication in other words can be said to be a method of exchanging information amongst one or many. John Adrin said that "communication is essentially the ability of one person to make himself or herself understand or, if you prefer, a slightly more formal version, communication is the process by which, meanings are exchanged between people through the use of a common set of symbols". Communication is a tool for exchanging views amongst one or many. He gives a definition in his book *Organisation Theory*: "Administrative Communication in a process which involves the transmission and accilates replication of ideas ensured by feedback for the purpose of eliciting actions which with accomplish organisational goals."

Types of Communication

Internal Communication

In order to prepare a layout in a company, internal communication is a must. It disseminates the goal of a company. It is through communication that a company prepares itself to achieve its goal, i.e., to gain profits. Human resources are organised in its best, i.e., creativity with efficiency. With the help of communication, members in the organisation select, develop and appraise its work ability. Communication motivates its workers to work hard. It not only directs but it also creates an environment in which people want to work and give their best. The performance of the workers is also controlled by communication.

External Communication

Communication between the enterprise and customer is mainly called external communication. It is due to external communication that the companies come to know about the products. The manufacturers can evaluate their product and if there are any flaws they can enhance their products. The organisation becomes an open system of interaction due to external communication. The organisation comes to know about their competitor as well as the treats and constraining factors.

Therefore, we can draw a conclusion that communication plays an important role in business world.

Methods of Communication

There are two types of communication:

Verbal Communication

They are of two types: oral and written

a) Oral Communication

It is very common and is the best way to communicate.

i) *Telephonic communication:* During a telephonic talk we must be very clear and specific so that the recipient is able to understand. We must not pun on the words or use similar sounding words at a stretch. We should not use sophisticated vocabulary and plain English so that the listener understands the message conveyed.

ii) *Face-to-face conversation*: It is the most common way of message transfer and most popular too. This sort of conversation is amongst two or a group of people. In this communication the recipient and the sender instantly come to know what are the plans of the other. The feedback is instant and hence the clarification is also on the spot. There are some basic needs for a face-to-face conversation. They are intonations, facial expressions, body language and tones.

iii) *Meeting*: Meeting are discussions over a fixed agenda. The chairperson of the meeting is responsible for the smooth undertaking of the meeting. Note making and minutes of the meeting are laid down in black and white which maintains an account of the meeting of undertaken.

iv) *Public speech*: In public speeches the recipient is far from the narrater /sender: Hence the senders' voice should be audible and clear so that his message to be imparted reaches the audience. A successful orator expresses himself with changing body language which enhances its speech. In public speeches the movement of hands and voice modulation can cast a deep impact upon the recipient. The voice modulation changes with emotions and sentiments.

v) *Interview*: A person appearing before a panel of people is known as an interviewee. The person facing the panel is tested for his ability and capability. Knowledge and professional skill are tested hand in hand.

vi) *Presentation*: The speaker prepares the speech on the topic given to him earlier. Presentation are formal talks. Presentations are knowledgeable and the audience are attentive to grasp from. The presenter must be a little humorous so that the audience are enthusiastic and interested during the presentation. Generally presentations are serious and diplomatic.

Presentations are made so that the customers /audience come to know the latest and correct information about the products of that company. To make the presentation more interactive and global audio/visual aids are taken. At the end of the presentation the audience asks the speaker their doubts about the presentation. Oral communication has its own merits. It saves money as well as time. The way in which one speaks is very influencing and effective and this helps in catching the attention of the audience.

We get feedback from the listeners instantly. Modulation of tone, intensity of voice affects the message put forward. In oral communication facial expressions and body language are important, and this affects the message conveyed.

For effective oral communication the voice should be clear and the pronunciation should be correct. The message imparted should be exact, brief and to the point. The idea's should be logically correct and we should maintain a sequence or a pattern. There should be simple and familiar words used in oral communication.

b) Written communication

There are many types of written communication, that is:

i) *Letter* : Letters are the most widely and popularly used written communication. This is used mainly for external communication. Letters have a format which must be followed.

ii) *Memo:* This is also a memorandum which helps in conveying interaction with workers; it may be used for brief messages. It is not necessary for the sender to sign the memo.

iii) *Report:* A report is a document collected by people on a given topic. In a report one collects, assembles and then presents the data in a proper format.

iv) *Circular:* A circular is a document which gives the details on a particular information or instruction. It has data, number and reference data too. A circular must be properly signed. They are mainly used in universal and government organisations.

v) *Minutes* : The solution or decision taken during meeting is jotted down in black and white and this written material is known as minuted. Minutes are legal papers.

Merits of written communication: The merit of written communication is that it can be referred again and again as everything is safely stored in written manner and thus it can used for future references as it is a legal and permanent record.

Non verbal communication

K. K.Seremo and E.M.Bodaclem defined non-verbal communication as, "Non-verbal communication refers to all external stimuli other than spoken or written words and including body in motions, characteristics of appearances, characteristics of voice and use of space and distancing." Summing up all the above ideas we get to know that non-verbal communication is mainly body language.

Singmerd Freud said, "He that has eyes to see and ears to hear may convince himself that no mortal can keep a secret. If his lips be silent he chats with fingertips and betrayal oozes out of him at every pore. Emotions and sentiments can be better expressed in non-verbal communication. There is famous saying that is silence speaks louder than words and that is what happens when one's body language are expressive.

There are two types of non-verbal communication:

Visual Method

1) *Colours*: Colours are the symbol of one's mood. The different colours symbolise different moods, like white for peace and purity, black for sorrow, red for danger. Colours also symbolise joy, fun, frolic. Bright colours excite people while dull and gloomy colours reduce one's enthusiasm.
2) *Posters*: Posters are mainly used for imparting social messages which are beneficial for all in general. They are also used as public visual aids.

3) *Pictures*: Pictures are again a vivid form of posters. In India a majority of the people are illiterate or semi-literate. Pictures and posters help the organisations to communicate with these people.

4) *Signs / Signals*: These are a more easy way to communicate with unknown people, like when we ask for a lift we show our thumb, as this is a signal for a lift. Traffic light signals are very popular it and used globally. Other globally used signals are waving one's hand while bidding goodbye, propagation of one's happiness by whistling, laughing at jokes, etc.

5) *Graphs / Charts / Maps, etc*: Graphs represent statistical inform, while maps represent tutorial information. Scales are very essential for all these three. Maps represent the vegetation, growth or area covered, wildlife area, populated area.

7) *Auditory* : Auditory signals are very less in number. They are whistles, buzzers, bells, etc. Buzzers are used in schools colleges, etc.

   Sirens are used by police vehicles; they are also used during war times to warn about enemies and raids. They are used as warning for fire or accidents. Whistles are used by police and army to assemble the members and convey different instructions. Trains and ships use whistle as a symbol of arrival or departure. People whistle when they are very happy.

8) *Tunes* : They are identified as work. The All India radio and television introduces its programs with special tunes and advertisements.

9) *Body Language*: The body language is the summation of facial expression, gestures, postures, movements, smell or touch, voice and sounds.

10) *Facial Expressions*: Facial expressions are the best way to communicate non-verbally. A person's emotions can hardly be hidden by facial expressions. The recipient can easily come to know about the feelings of the sender. Although a person may not agree to it yet

expressions say most of it. Therefore, we can conclude that emotions never contradict verbal statement. Eye contact is necessary when two people are talking to each other.

11) *Gestures/Postures/Movements*:- Postures and body movement indicate how we think about ourselves, and how others relate to us. We maintain good postures mostly like head held up straight, standing straight with feets close.

    Behaviourists have identified three types of shapes of our bodies.

    i) *Ectomorph*: Thin, youthful and tall.

    ii) *Mesomorph*: Strong, athletic, muscular.

    iii) *Endomorph*: Fat, round and soft.

    This is a fact that our postures do communicate a lot about us, like what kind of person we are, what are our likes and dislikes.

12). *Smell and Touch*: People through touch convey their warmth and feeling to the recipient. A pat on the back or on the cheek is promoted by various emotions.

13) *Voice and Sound*: The voice made by the speaker while speaking is also a part of non-verbal communication which is known as a paralanguage or paraliguistic. For example, the words, "What a fine day!" could be a compliment but if the tone of the voice is sarcastic and said in order to blast, the true meaning is anger.

Functions of Communication

Information

To provide information to organisation about its product is the main function of communication. Firstly, information is to collect data from all sources, i.e., through media, verbal and non-verbal, body language, audio/visual aids, newspapers and journals, advertisement and many more sources. Thus the information is collected from all the sources and this information is passed to the organisation where they analyse and evaluate the data. The policy of the organisation is formed only when the information has been received.

Control

There are many people working in the enterprise and we know that everyone has his own behaviour of working, hence proper control becomes important. There are formed rules and regulations of every company which is to be followed by the employee now-a-days informal communication is more effective and more popular than formal communication.

Motivation

According to *Collins Cobalt's Dictionary*, "If you are motivated to do something, you are caused to feel determined to achieve something and willing to work hard in order to succeed. So you have to first motivate the children and then to teach them." This also goes on with the workers. If the company promotes and encourages its workers and shows it concern toward them then the workers would like to put in their best effort for the company.

Emotional Intelligence

As we know, communication is a social activity, and in an organisation; it is a social entity; hence the people who comprise the society have so much to share in an organisation and pass them. Golman says, "emotional intelligence is to do with how well we manage our own inner lives and get along with people." Stephen Coray says, "Creative and the unity necessary to run a business or a family or a marriage requires great personal strength and courage. No amount of technical administrative skills in labouring for the masses can make up for the lack of nobility of personal character in developing relationship. It is a very essential one-to-one level that we have the loss of love and life."

Importance of Communication

An organisation is a place where people are working at different levels. They all have there own opinions and approaches. For a common profit all the different people must join hands together. In today's world of technical advancement a lot of importance is given to effective communication skills.

The dominance of English in the administrative world is still prevalent and therefore we have to focus our attention conversation in English in India.

Hence we can say that English is a language of technocrats.

Index